Aruna Chakravarti has been principal of a prestigious women's college of Delhi University for ten years. She is also a well-known academic, creative writer and translator with seventeen published books to her name. They comprise five novels, two books of short stories, two academic works and eight volumes of translation.

Her first novel *The Inheritors* (published by Penguin Random House) was shortlisted for the Commonwealth Writers' Prize and her second, *Jorasanko* (published by HarperCollins) received critical acclaim and also became a bestseller. *Daughters of Jorasanko* (HarperCollins), a sequel to *Jorasanko*, has sold widely and received rave reviews. Her novel *Suralakshmi Villa*, published by Pan Macmillan Ltd under the Picador imprint, has been adjudged 'Novel of the year (India 2020)' by *Indian Bibliography* published in *The Journal of Commonwealth Literature U.K.* Her latest novel, *The Mendicant Prince,* a semi-fictional account of the Bhawal legal case, was released by Pan Macmillan Ltd, in July 2022 to widespread media coverage and acclaim. Her second book of short stories *Through a Looking Glass: Stories* was also released the same year by Om Books International Ltd. Two other books are in the publication process and will be released this year.

Her translated works include an anthology of songs from Rabindranath Tagore's *Gitabitaan,* Saratchandra Chattopadhyay's *Srikanta* and Sunil Gangopadhyay's *Those Days, First Light* and *Primal Woman: Stories.*

Among the various awards she has received are Vaitalik Award, Sahitya Akademi Award and Sarat Puraskar.

She is also a scriptwriter and producer of seven multi-media presentations based on her novels. Comprising dramatized readings, interspersed with songs and accompanied by a visual presentation by professional artists and singers, these programmes have been widely acclaimed and performed in many parts of India and abroad.

Praise for the Book

'Aruna Chakravarti sets off to search for stories that reflect the life and longings of Dalit women. An accomplished translator, she picks from both Dalit and non-Dalit writers and gives us a fascinating bouquet of twelve stories. In today's India, where voices from the margins are coming centre-stage, this is a worthy endeavour. The collection includes voices of Dalit writers themselves besides some accomplished writers such as Saratchandra who observe from the outside. An interesting collage.'

—Saba Naqvi, author and journalist

'This anthology of Dalit stories, sensitively translated and edited by Aruna Chakravarti, reflects her depth of understanding of a relatively less discussed reality of Bengal: the Dalit existence at the margins. The editor's deep insight and diligent research has brought in writing by contemporary Dalit writers like Manoranjan Byapari, Kalyani Thakur and Nakul Mallik in the same literary continuum as Saratchandra, Tarashankar Bandyopadhyay, Prafulla Ray and Mahasweta Devi.

'Writing about underprivileged life has been a part of Bengal's rich literary tradition. Yet, stories about lives which spring from Dalit consciousness have rarely been acknowledged in the literary history of Bengal where class, and not caste, remains the primary identity.

'Even today, the life of a Dalit is steeped in poverty as most of them are landless and in socially marginalised low-income professions. Many Dalit women are severely exploited. Their labour is mostly unpaid or underpaid and they are vulnerable as objects of physical exploitation. Stories in this volume bring out their anguish, rebellion, and courage to take on society. The collection will stand out as a valuable literary and social documentation.'

—Anita Agnihotri, bureaucrat and writer

'Aruna Chakravarti is a distinguished educationist, creative writer, translator and much more. None of this, however, prepares you for the power and horror of her voice in her latest work *Rising from the Dust*. This is a book that not only exposes the brutality endured by women from the most oppressed castes of Bengal but shouts out, howls and weeps with anguish. Simultaneously, it describes magical moments that light up the lives of even the most desolate. The lingering taste of curried fish that melts in the mouth; the fragrance emanating from a pot of fresh hot rice; the wind passing over silver water in the moonlight; the sense of power that revenge brings, however momentary.'

—Subhashini Ali, politician

'The meticulous attention to detail of language that reflects the Dalit act of remembering the heinous insults piled on them is reflected in *Rising from the Dust*, Aruna Chakravarti's translation of Dalit stories from Bengal. The stories have stunning metaphors and descriptions. There is so much richness in the language even in translation.'

—*The Telegraph*

Selected and Translated by
Aruna Chakravarti

RISING FROM THE DUST

Dalit Stories from Bengal

Om Books International

First published in 2025 by

Om Books International

Corporate & Editorial Office
A-12, Sector 64, Noida 201 301
Uttar Pradesh, India
Phone: +91 120 477 4100
Email: editorial@ombooks.com
Website: www.ombooksinternational.com

Sales Office
107, Ansari Road, Darya Ganj,
New Delhi 110 002, India
Phone: +91 11 4000 9000
Email: sales@ombooks.com
Website: www.ombooks.com

ISBN: 978-93-6395-320-8

Printed in India

10 9 8 7 6 5 4 3 2 1

To my youngest brother Arun with much affection…

Contents

Foreword: Meena Kandasamy xiii

Translator's Note xvii

1. **The Fortress** (*Durgo*): *Manoranjan Byapari* 1
2. **Salt** (*Labanakto*): *Bimalendu Haldar* 11
3. **The True Life Story of Uli-Buli's Mother** (*Uli-Buli-r Ma-er Jebon Beetyanto*): *Mahasweta Devi* 33
4. **Nalini's Story** (*Nolini-r Upakhyan*): *Mahasweta Devi* 40
5. **Shonkhomala** (*Shonkhomala*): *Manohar Mouli Biswas* 62
6. **Snake Maiden** (*Naagmati*): *Prafulla Kumar Roy* 72
7. **Illegal Immigrant** (*Anuprabeshkari*): *Nakul Mallik* 111
8. **The Witch** (*Daini*): *Tarashankar Bandyopadhyay* 127
9. **Raikamal** (*Raikamal*): *Tarashankar Bandyopadhyay* 153
10. **Motho's Daughter** (*Motho-r Maiyya*): *Kalyani Thakur Charal* 172
11. **Abhagi's Heaven** (*Abhagi-r Swarga*): *Saratchandra Chattopadhyay* 178
12. **The Insect Festival** (*Poka Parbon*): *Anil Ghorai* 196

Notes on Contributors 224

Let me forget that I was born in the dust;
there is no dust within me…
—*Chandalika*, **Rabindranath Tagore**

Foreword

Meena Kandasamy

I consider it an honour to be writing this foreword to Dr Aruna Chakravarti's translation of Bengali short stories that encapsulate a world of Dalit experience, resistance, and resilience. Every short story in this collection holds together a precious, precarious universe—the old order continues with its oppression, the new is struggling to be born; everyday life is a struggle and yet, struggle itself is the terrain where life, liveliness, and being alive come into their full glory.

The women in this book are exceptional. Chintay in Bimalendu Haldar's 'Salt', Sarama in Manoranjan Byapari's 'Fortress' and Nalini in Mahasweta Devi's 'Nalini's Story' are some of the feisty women you will encounter in these pages—their natural tendency to challenge authority and face adversity is admirable. The dialectics of survival and social ostracization are explored with nuanced sensitivity in every story, reflecting the complex contradictions which arise in the tensions between upheaval and oppression. This book is an immersive reading experience—capturing the essence of a way of life that is marked by the enduring defiant spirit of the dispossessed and the marginalized. The choice of the translator to place stories about the Dalit condition written by Mahasweta Devi, alongside a story by Manoranjan Byapari, whose work she first published in her print magazine *Bortika*, allows for literary history to come full circle.

I vividly remember going through issues of the *Economic and Political Weekly* while trying to research my first novel, and being thoroughly distracted when I came across the bold, provocative title of an essay: "Is There Dalit Writing in Bangla?" In this short piece, Meenakshi Mukherjee introduced and translated Manoranjan Byapari, who in turn introduced and situated the history of Dalit writing in Bangla. It is a beautiful and intimate stand-out essay, and trying to write this introduction, I went to the digital archives to find the piece (it's from 2007). Byapari finishes his remarkable essay with the reflection that 'Dalit literature in Bangla can no longer be wished away or consigned to invisibility or relegated to the margins. Whether one likes it or not, this sapling has taken root in the soil.'

I was able to read Byapari's own writings through Arunava Sinha's brilliant, impeccable translations: *There's Gunpowder in the Air* (*Batashe Baruder Gandha*, Leftword Books) and *Imaan* (Eka). Looking at Bangla Dalit writing as a complex, composite whole, I also encourage readers to pick up the recent anthology *Under My Dark Skin Flows a Red River: Translations of Dalit Writings from Bengal* (Samya).

In this iconic essay, Byapari laments, that despite a 'large crop of short stories by Bengali Dalit writers' they are 'hardly noticed by the literary establishment of Kolkata'. He does not name the self-evident malaise which cause this literary malaise. In the shadow of his astute, acute observation, Dr Chakravarti's initiative to put together this volume shows that redressal is possible.

Dr Chakravarti's translation—meticulous, exacting, effortless—keeps the flavours of Bengali alive, and to translate a language in all its iterations and moodiness is no mean feat. She has imbibed the text with rich sensory detail, retained local words and idiomatic expressions, and allowed the reader to be anchored in the cultural backdrop of every story. I congratulate her for putting together this volume.

Translator's Note

People often ask me why I continue translating when my own creative writing is so well received by readers. That's because moving from creative writing to translation, from time to time, is a refreshing change for me. Since the novels I write are usually historical or biographical, the writing process invariably carries with it a certain amount of tension and anxiety pertaining to fact and authenticity. In consequence, I breathe a sigh of relief after completing a novel, and take up a work of translation which brings me all the enjoyment of creative writing minus the worry and misgivings. Though this is not a rule ... it happens quite often.

After writing *The Mendicant Prince* which involved intense research and analysis of nineteenth-century social conditions especially as they pertained to women, the family history of the Bhawals and legal and medical records of the case, I decided to get together an anthology of stories focusing on the plight of Dalit women in Bengal and translate them into English.

The idea came to me after reading a biography of Rani Rasmoni. The oppression and humiliation that Dalits have suffered for centuries is being recognized today and a whole body of literature has emerged in the wake of this recognition. But, as it seems to me, Dalits are being looked at as a homogeneous group by most writers. The fact is that there are divisions and subdivisions even within the Dalit community and some castes are more sinned against than others. Another thing—women suffer from a double stigma. Their caste as well as their gender go against them. The injustice and persecution that Dalit women battle, day in and day out, need to be highlighted more intensely than is being done.

Hindu society has been structured in a way that makes poverty a given in the lives of the lower castes. However, poverty is a lesser evil, at least in Bengal. The soil is fertile and varieties of wild fruits, tubers and greens can be found in forests and along the banks of rivers. There are many waterbodies which teem with fish in certain seasons. Consequently food, barring exceptional times, is not very difficult to access. But women, with their natural instinct for nurturing and conditioned by societal expectations, give their husbands and children whatever is available, keeping only the scrapings in the pot for themselves. This leads to severe malnutrition and early death in wives and mothers.

But an even bigger affliction they face is their treatment as chattels, not only by their families but by society at large. Violence, abuse, rape and being robbed of their possessions by powerful men, is still an accepted norm in the obscurer villages of Bengal. But how many writers have recorded this special dilemma or are representing it in their writing today? If Rani Rasmoni had to suffer the indignities she did because she was a Shudra, how much worse life would have been for the ordinary woman of her community?

I first thought of taking up Rabindranath Tagore's *Chandalika*, one of the most sensitive explorations of a Chandal woman's psyche that I have come across. But I changed my mind. A collection of stories would be a better idea, I thought. I started looking and was pleasantly surprised at finding some excellent representations of the Dalit woman's angst in both Dalit and non-Dalit Bengali writing. Unfortunately, many of these stories have not been translated into English and are therefore inaccessible to an international readership. I am delighted that the idea came to me. Translating these stories has given me a sense of fulfilment I've seldom felt before.

People ask me on what basis I chose the stories contained in this volume. Were there some special criteria that had to be followed? Or any pressing commitment that needed to be honoured? No. There was nothing of the sort. I chose these stories because I liked them. Besides, I wanted the anthology to span an entire century of writing that explores the Dalit woman's cause and holds it up to the light. It explains the inclusion of stories by novelists like Saratchandra Chattopadhyay, Tarashankar Bandyopadhyay, Mahasweta Devi and Prafulla Roy. They weren't Dalits but their profound understanding of the Dalit woman's fears and traumas, hopes, dreams and aspirations, shakes the reader both intellectually and emotionally, to this day. I also wanted my readers to hear the voices of contemporary writers from the Dalit community. Fresh, new voices revealing astonishing potential. Manoranjan Byapari, Bimalendu Haldar, Manohar Mouli Biswas, Kalyani Thakur Charal, Anil Ghorai and Nakul Mallik are some of the brightest stars in the literary firmament of Bengal today and the stories contained in this volume are some of their best ones.

The Fortress

Manoranjan Byapari

Night falls. Stealthy and brooding like a waiting assailant. Poised for attack. All Sarama's eyes can see are wave upon wave of impenetrable darkness. The man enters the room. His form is erect; his step bold. He peels the clothes off her body with practised hands. A butcher skinning a goat. Forcing her to the ground he sits on her soft breasts.

Drub ... Drub... Drub. Rhythmic movements. Swift and hard. Swifter and harder...

Sarama doesn't make a sound. Sound is sin.

Another enters. Swims into her womb. A third, a fourth, a fifth...

The neighbours sleep in peace. It needs courage to keep awake. So ... they sleep.

Sarama is silent. Sound has abandoned her.

Long after the forms have melted away, she sits up. 'O Ma go!' she groans in pain. 'Water!' She slithers on her stomach like a snake towards the water pot. It is empty. Dry as dust. She crawls into the yard. Loses her way...

⋆

Sarama had been turned into a widow in a single night. The night her sack of sindoor sank into the foetid, festering waters of the canal. It rose to the surface three days later. From that day Sarama became everyone's concern.

It isn't right. Panchanan Koyal's considered opinion. *Eight kotahs of land at the crossroads! Prime property! Owned by a single woman! Why?*

One day he calls Sarama and shares his concern. 'Look, Sarama,' he counsels, 'you have this fine healthy body. Why waste it in selling dung cakes? Go to the town. You will live like a queen.'

'What about my land?'

'I'll give you something for it.'

'It's ancestral land. My husband's forefathers…'

Panchanan shakes his head. He is saddened.

One day Panchanan's desire gets official recognition. Big man Barda accepts his explanation. *Toady!*

'A woman?'

'She's Nakul Duley's widow.'

'Which Nakul?'

'The one who was charged guilty of…'

'Do as you wish,' Older and wiser Barda cautions. 'But be careful…'

A few days later a police summons reaches Sarama. She is to appear at Panchanan Koyal's house at once.

'When are you leaving the village?' Flashes of lightning illumine Panchanan's teeth.

'Where shall I go?'

'To hell. You won't be allowed to live here.'

'Why not?'

'Your presence is damaging the purity of the village. Our young men are losing their characters.'

This Panchanan was not the old Panchanan. The one who had tried to persuade her with flattery. Even offered money for her land. He was a strong man now. Behind him were a hundred men with lathis.

'When are you getting out? I need to know.'

'Why are you after me? What have I done? Have I robbed your house? Or set it on fire?'

'You are Nakul's widow. He was a criminal.'

The heat was unbearable. The sun's beams as sharp as a thousand spears. The air was thick with poisonous fumes.

'When will you go?'

Suddenly, dead Nakul speaks in Sarama's voice. 'I won't go.'

Panchanan stares at Sarama. Sarama stares at Panchanan.

'Is that your last word?'

'Yes.'

Panchanan adds two and two together and completes the sum.

She has to be taught a lesson.

*

With the fall of dusk, bricks and stones come hurtling onto Sarama's roof. Her milch cow tosses and groans all night and dies the next morning. The fish in her pond float on the surface, bloated bellies turned to the sky. A good meal of Follidol? The neighbours click their tongues in sympathy. Panchanan sniggers.

'Is this right?' a man, with chaff in place of a brain, questions worriedly.

He has to be silenced. He's a toady.

'Eight kotahs of land!' the fool persists.

'Who says so?'

He can't take names. Taking names is dangerous. Arguing is dangerous too. His mouth shuts with a snap.

Panchanan is the acknowledged headman of the district. He has connections and contacts in the upper echelons. His word is law. And Sarama? She is Nakul's widow. The same Nakul who had a case filed against him. The protest dissolves in the man's throat.

A friend of Nakul is Panchanan's left-hand man these days. He is known as Mejo Babu. He meets Sarama in secret.

'What will you do now?'

'You tell me.'

'You are in danger. Grave danger.'

'You know best.'

'My advice is … *Let go.*'

'Do I have anything left to hold on to?'

'Your character. Your prestige.'

'I thought you had human feelings,' Sarama's mouth curls in contempt. 'I'm speaking, of course, of another time.'

'It's difficult … A human being protests when he sees injustice. And that endangers him. It is better to let humanity go to sleep. It is even better to sell it. You gain something then. Name and fame and money. You have power over others. That's why I'm telling you…'

'To go away?'

'Yes.'

'Where shall I go?'

'Anywhere. Don't stay in this village. You have no one of your own here.'

'Where do I have someone of my own?'

The man looks up startled. He is speechless. His sympathy for her receives a rude jolt. He has tried to help her. But…

He walks away.

Sarama sits and broods. Her limbs are young and lissom. Rippling with sweet sap. Like the musk deer, she is driven wild by her own scent.

The next scene is stained with dirt and blood. Men barge into her house. Strip her layer by layer and go out. Tell her they will come again.

Morning dawns. Neighbours crowd at her door. They form three groups.

The members of the first group click their tongues. *A ha … A ha*. Doleful mutterings.

Ha! Ha! Ha! Roars of laughter from the second.

The third lot is silent.

'Why didn't you shout for help?' one from the *A ha* group.

'What good would it have done?' another from the same.

'If everyone came out together…'

'Who's everyone?'

Silence.

'But something needs to be done,' the first one persists.

Sarama stares at them. Her ears are filled with sound. Meaningless sound.

She rises and pushes her way out of the crowd. Walks step by step towards Panchanan's house.

'Why are you doing this to me?'

'What have *I* done?' Panchanan doesn't know what it is to be angry. He is a model of patience and calm. 'I explained everything to you, Sarama. You chose not to listen.'

'I'm going to the police.'

'Very well. Go.'

*

Not that day. Not even the next. On the third day a police jeep drives up to Panchanan's house. Inspector Saheb steps out and walks in. He returns to the station convinced that *to forgive is the highest of human virtues.* And Panchanan's faith in the Chief's deference to his wishes is justified anew. Sarama has no idea of what has gone on there.

Days go by. Nights close in. Sarama holds conversations with the dark these days. She asks questions and receives grimaces in reply.

Bitter hate, conceived in the innermost womb of Panchanan's soul, swells with dynamic life. His nails turn into claws; his teeth into fangs.

Sarama's life is unbearable these days. Thousands of eyes lick her form with slavering tongues. The *Ha Ha* group lurks under the silk cotton tree, all day, waiting to pounce on her. *There she goes. Look there ... there.* Shouts of laughter. Drunken leers. She runs away from the light and buries her face in the dark. But the dark is cruel too. Her soul is torn from her body in tiny shreds. Silence everywhere. Deep silence. Silence chokes her. Protest, like an opium eater, sleeps in her breast. She burns. *She is burned...*

Silence is shattered by sound. Elation bursts out of the throats of doms, like skulls rupturing on flaming pyres. Arms, stretching from the mountains to the sea, encircle her. Bind her with iron shackles...

Out in the fields, collecting cow dung, she sees eyes. Naked eyes graze her neck. Lash at her limbs. Her body streams with sweat. She is like a muniya bird caught in a trap. She flutters her wings. Struggles to free herself.

Eyes, dark and malevolent, creep towards her. Come closer and closer. Beneath her back the burning earth crashes and splinters. Eyes feast on her. Drool and dribble. Suck and slurp. Drain every drop. Leave her dry and brittle as chewed sugarcane.

The tiger doesn't bother to vanquish his enemy. Jackals do it for him. The sun in the sky is witness...

Sarama weeps. The heat of an angry summer dries her tears. Volcanoes erupt in her eyes.

'Don't you have mothers and sisters?'

No answer. She is alone. Lying in a deserted field. Naked in the light of a scorching sun.

Panchanan is a contented man these days. His worry over the eight kotahs of land has been laid to rest. His gang of toadies are ecstatic. Sarama has become a public woman. Acknowledged. Undisputed. Anyone can enjoy her now.

*

On her way home that evening, a basketful of cow dung on her head, she meets Ratan's wife Parul. Ratan is a rickshaw driver in the village of Nabhasan.

'You here?'

'*Hunh*. Fate has played a cruel trick on me, Didi. My husband can't work anymore.'

'Why? What's wrong?'

'He's suffering from a disease that even the gods can't cure. He contracted it in town when driving his rickshaw.'

'What disease?'

Parul is silent for a few minutes. 'A shameful one, Didi,' she mutters. Taking a deep breath she continues slowly, 'Poison women! Haven't you seen them, all decked in tinsel, standing here and there in the bazar? Under the paint and glitter their skins ooze deadly venom. To touch them is to die. My fool husband courted death. He's dying.'

Bitter rage contorts Parul's face as she utters these words. Her hair stands on end like flames. Her eyes turn into rivers. 'I've run away and come to my parents. Why should I share his shame and die with him?'

Parul walks away. Sarama stands in the middle of the path watching her. Her head is on fire. Fire under the soles of her feet. Flames leap and dance in her mind.

She comes home. Bathes for a long time. Twines her hair into a knot high on her head. Lines her eyes with kajal. Wears a red-and-green striped sari. Tucks the folds neatly into her petticoat. Shrugging off all shame she steps on to the road. Nabhasan isn't too far away.

*

Ratan's emaciated form is barely visible on the bed. The room is empty; the silence eerie. The heat of the day has softened with the setting sun.

'You?' Ratan's eyes are fogged; their light dimmed with a yellow haze. *Is it a dream? No. It is Sarama. But why?*

Ratan … ten years ago. He and Sarama. Weddings and feasts. Song and dance. Fairs and festivals. They were young and pristine then. Unblemished.

'How are you?' A pained smile on Ratan's lips. Like the flutter of leaves in a storm.

'Not well.' A sigh rises from deep within Sarama's chest. She feels her ribs cracking with pain.

'I've heard.'

'So have I.'

Two pairs of eyes gaze on one another. They ask the same question.

Why did this happen to us? Why do such things happen?

Sarama sits beside the sick man. *This room, this bed, this man could have been mine. Would I have run away like Parul? To save myself?*

Hate? Yes. She would seethe and boil with hate. Rage and revulsion would set her limbs on fire. Corrode her soul. She would feed the fire and bask in it. But she wouldn't run away…

Time flows like a stream. The sun has set. Dusk has crept into the corners of the room. The air is chill and dark. Like the inside of a coffin.

'Will you do me a favour?' Sarama's voice is a whisper.

'Favour? *I* do *you* a favour?' Ratan, standing on the brink of extinction, asks with his eyes.

'Give me one night,' Sarama's lips murmur.

Has Sarama gone mad? Can a thirst for vengeance drive a woman completely insane?

'I want one night from you. Only one.'

Ratan's soul is shaken to its foundations. Someone is gripping his throat with iron fingers.

'What are you?' A hiss escapes his lips.

Sarama looks at him with feral eyes. She has metamorphosed. From woman to predatory beast. She is a tigress … ruthless in her revenge.

Suddenly the mask cracks into shards. Falls to her feet. 'Save me,' she cries out piteously and bursts into tears.

The old adulterous blood leaps up in Ratan's veins. His passion for female flesh, long spent and forgotten, bursts into flame. He sits up. Leans towards her. She strokes his neck. Places her lips on his. Sucks the venom out of him with a long, stinging, shuddering kiss.

She comes home late at night. She is a pot brimming over with poison. She leaves her door open. Locks and latches are redundant now. She doesn't need protection. Her body has become a fortress. The God of Death resides within its walls. Ready to strike. He knows no mercy. No forgiveness.

Sarama's mind and body glow like a furnace. Venom has driven out fear. She will welcome every touch. Invite them. She waits outside her door in delicious anticipation…

Salt

Bimalendu Haldar

Three days have gone by since the fire in Chintay's kitchen has been lit. Three days since her man went out with his nets at night and didn't return. Three days and three nights Chintay has been worrying and fretting…

Chintay's real name is Chintamoni but everyone calls her Chintay. She and her husband Madhai live in a mud hut in the village of Sonakhali on a bank of the Matla in Canning. They have no children. Madhai catches fish from the Matla in Nishay Ghosh's boat and is paid a daily wage. And Chintay buys phyansa, amudi, lotay and bhola from the fish market in Canning, then takes the 6 a.m. local train to Sonarpur and sells the fish there. She comes home around three o'clock in the afternoon. Madhai has returned long before her, eaten a bellyful of last night's leftover rice, spread a mat in the courtyard and fallen asleep snoring like a buffalo.

Chintay cooks the one meal of the day and wakes Madhai up. They eat together. By the time Chintay has finished all her other chores dusk has fallen and it is time for Madhai to pick up his nets and go out on his nightly mission…

That morning Chintay had bought some ilish along with her phyansa, bhola and other cheap fish. They were about fifteen in number, small in size, the type babus call khoka ilish. Khoka ilish appears in the Matla during the autumn season. Chintay had kept the largest and freshest one aside. She wouldn't sell it. She would go home and cook it into a tasty jhol with chunks of aubergine. She had bought three kilos of *dudh-er sawr*, a fragrant white rice, from Sonarpur market yesterday. *Dudh-er sawr bhaat* and *Ilish-er jhol!* Aah! The saliva squirted into her mouth at the thought. She loved ilish.

It wasn't as if she and Madhai didn't get to eat fish. They did. The bland, tasteless, cheap fish and shrimps that were left unsold in Chintay's basket appeared in her cooking wok every day. Madhai was also given a share of the fish he had caught, by Nishay Ghosh. But he rarely brought it home. Most days he sold it in Canning market and spent the money on toddy. On his return, he would tell Chintay that Nishay Ghosh hadn't given him any fish that day. Chintay knew he was lying but didn't say so to his face. She preferred to keep a discreet silence.

But it was the ilish season now and for the last few days she had been urging him to bring home his share of the fish he would catch. But Madhai wasn't only a liar. He was stubborn, aggressive, and a toddy addict. Turning a deaf ear to her pleas he continued selling it and blowing the money on toddy.

Chintay came home that afternoon to find it empty. Madhai hadn't returned. The lock hung crookedly from the sheet of bamboo slips that was their front door. Entering the yard, she found a stray dog lying curled up in the corner where Madhai used to sleep. The yard was littered with animal droppings and the stench of goat urine blew in her face. Two hens, she didn't know whose they were, pecked contentedly at the fish scales and vegetable peelings in the ash heap. She went into the kitchen, a flimsy structure of dried grass and wattle, and looked around. Everything was in place. Exactly as she had left it that morning. Nothing had been touched. The sour, pungent smell of rotting rice and fish curry pervaded the air. That meant Madhai hadn't come home that day. Strange! Where was the man and what was he up to?

Chintay's brows came together. What would she do now? Where would she go looking for her husband? Nishay Ghosh's warehouse was in Canning Bazar. She could go there and enquire. But Nishay Ghosh would have locked the door by now and left for his home in Henrhodanga village where he went every afternoon for his midday meal and siesta. He would return only after dusk. Should she go to the men who had sailed with Madhai last night? They might know where he was.

Nishay Ghosh sent out his boats twice a day. Once at crack of dawn and once at night. He had four boats with four men manning each. One at the helm, one plying the oars, and two fishermen. Of all his men Madhai was the most efficient and experienced. He could, in an emergency, even steer and row a boat. But he was the only one who lived in Sonakhali. The others, Phatik Danrhi, Jainal Majhi and Ruhit Jeley lived in Henrhodanga and Nikarighata. Those villages were very far away. To reach them one had to catch the ferry from Canning, then walk several miles. But Chintay had never been there and didn't know the way. To go wandering in search of Madhai's boat mates wouldn't be an easy task. Much better to wait till evening for Nishay Ghosh's return.

The village of Sonakhali ran along one bank of the Matla for a couple of miles, curving somewhat like an elephant's trunk. At the tip a group of fisher folk had built a cluster of hovels taking care to maintain a safe distance from the houses of the upper castes. They eked out a miserable existence. Men, women and children lived cramped within crumbling walls of mud and wattle with hens and ducks, sheep and goats, nets and baskets, ropes and knives, rags and cooking pots. The men went out fishing in the boats of the warehouse owners through rain, wind and storm. The work was hard and dangerous and their masters got richer by the day. But all they received in return for their labour was a paltry daily wage. Not enough to give them and their families two square meals a day. The women caught small fish, crabs and shrimps from the shallower waters. Carrying the day's catch in baskets on their heads they walked for miles and sold it in the surrounding villages. Chintay and Madhai had built their hut at the furthest edge of the cluster. Beyond it was the river and a stretch of paddy field. And even beyond were other villages.

Chintay decided to begin her search from the village itself. First, she went to the shrines of the tribal goddesses Bonbibi and Manasa. Madhai wasn't there as she knew he wouldn't. Next, she walked along the dyke, crossed the bus stand and auto stand and peeped into all the toddy shops. No sign of Madhai. She stood, nonplussed, for a while. *What next?* She decided to go home and wait for evening. If Nishay Ghosh had some information ... well and good. If not, she would take the ferry to Henrhodanga tomorrow morning and look for Madhai's boat mates. And if even they...?

Chintay's heart missed a beat. Her head swam and she felt faint. She hadn't eaten anything since dawn. Only two nehrho biscuits and a cup of tea from the teashop in Sonarpur Bazar. She hadn't bathed either. Her body was coated with dust and her head felt hot and dry. But she couldn't think of a bath or food just now. She couldn't think of anything...

She sat leaning against one of the bamboo posts that held up the thatch of her hut with a vacant look in her eyes. The day was drawing to a close. There was still some light in the west and a few shreds of reddish cloud were floating in the sky. Two crows were shrieking from a branch of the hog plum tree that grew in her yard. She could see the river from where she sat. A flock of sparrows flitted in and out of the bushes of bani and keora that grew by the bank twittering merrily. A sweet breeze blew.

The basket she had brought home lay in a corner of the yard. Two cats were fighting over the lotay and ilish she had planned to cook that day. They were spitting and snarling at each other. She glanced at the scene and turned her eyes away. What was the use of shooing them away? She wouldn't cook the fish or eat it...

She couldn't sit still anymore. Rising to her feet she made her way to the ferry ghat. She would go to Kusho Sardar's house first, she decided. Kusho Sardar, like Madhai, went fishing in a boat belonging to another warehouse owner. He might be able to help her. But Kusho hadn't even heard that her husband hadn't returned that morning. He gave her a piece of news, though. Madhai and his mates had taken their boat deep into the Sundarbans last night. There was a rumour afloat that ilish was appearing in shoals at the bend of the river near Saatmukho. It was a dangerous venture but Madhai had decided to attempt it.

Chintay made her way carefully down the dyke and stepped on the bank. The tide hadn't come in yet and the ground had turned into a quagmire. She was afraid she would be sucked in any moment into the sea of swirling mud. A strong wind blew in her face. Above her head, the sky was covered with scudding clouds. They had been red a while ago but were fast fading to ash. They could turn black any moment and send down a volley of showers. That was the problem with the autumn season.

One never knew when it would rain and when it wouldn't. If she got caught in the rain she would be in deep trouble.

'*Ki lo,* Chintay!' A woman's voice called from behind. 'Where are you off to at this unearthly hour?' Chintay turned around. It was Haran's mother. Haran's mother, like her, made a living by buying and selling fish. But she didn't sell in Canning or the neighbouring villages. She caught the vegetable train at the crack of dawn, every morning to Kolkata, and sold her wares in Baithakkhana bazar where she got a better price.

'To Nishay Ghosh's warehouse, Khurhi,' Chintay answered.

'What takes you there?' The old woman frowned. 'That, too, so late in the evening?'

'Your nephew hasn't returned from last night's fishing. Nishay Ghosh will know the reason.'

'*Ma go!* What could have happened? Madhai is a good boy. Steady and responsible. Have you made enquiries in the village?'

'It's the first thing I did.'

'*Hunh*! Our boys have all gone wild chasing ilish these days. It's possible that Madhai went further down the river than he meant to and got stuck somewhere. He's sure to be back tomorrow morning.'

'It's what I think too, Khurhi.'

'That must be it. Don't worry. All will be well. Let me know when he returns.'

*

Nishay Ghosh's warehouse stood high on the dyke, beyond the jetty. It wasn't very impressive. Three sheets of garan and hetal leaves woven together, then plastered with mud, formed the walls. The front was made of wooden planks with a door and a window. The roof was corrugated tin. It was quite large inside. There was a bed in it and a few articles of daily use. The walls were lined with shelves on which fish was stored in bamboo trays. But they were empty now. A gigantic pair of scales stood in the middle of the room with a bench next to it. It was for buyers to sit while ordering the day's supply. Chintay had come to the warehouse quite often before, but today there was something different about it. It was filled with people. Not buyers. People like herself. Three fishwives squatted on the floor with a swarm of children clinging to their saris. Nishay Ghosh sat on a wooden chair facing them with his back to the light. She couldn't see his face properly. But she sensed the unease radiating from him and enveloping everyone in the room.

'Here's another!' Nishay Ghosh glared at her and shouted angrily, 'Listen, every one of you. I won't take this lying down. I'll whale the living daylights out of each one...'

Chintay was shocked out of her wits. *Why was the master shouting? What had happened?* Now Nishay Ghosh's right-hand man came forward with an explanation. Madhai, Ruhit, Phatik and Jainal had gone out last night, as usual, and hadn't come back. The other fishermen, who had returned safe and sound, had reported that Madhai and his mates had taken their boat to the 'big river' near Saatmukho. But they had done so without Nishay Ghosh's permission. It was the master's firm belief that they hadn't gone in search of ilish. They had sold the boat and nets, which were brand new, and were spending the money on toddy and women. They would come back tomorrow with a carefully spun yarn about dacoits attacking the boat and they escaping with their bare lives. But Nishay Ghosh was not a fool. He had already lodged a complaint in the local thana against all four. He would wait a day or two for their return, then decide what to do next.

Chintay glanced at the women sitting on the floor. Their faces were tense and anxious and streaked with tears. The man who had been speaking on the master's behalf introduced them to her. Phatik's wife was a thin dark girl in a tattered filthy sari. Her name was Palani. A mane of coarse tangled hair hung down her back. Her skin was so dry … it looked as though it had been dusted with chalk. She had a little boy of about two with her, stark naked, with a tiny bird body, so frail … his bones stuck out of his skin, sharp as thorns. Mucus dripped out of his nostrils in thick, fat, clingy drops.

Jainal's wife was called Zubeida. She wasn't as dark as Palani. Her skin was the colour of copper. She wore a striped cotton sari, soiled at the hem and stitched together in places. She too had a child with her, a little girl with a bit of flimsy cloth hanging from her waist. Her nose was clean but thick viscous liquid ran down her eyes in streams.

Ruhit Jeley's wife Tagar looked somewhat better than the other two. Like Chintay she was short and squat with a firm healthy body and a smooth dark skin. She had two boys with her. The older one wore underpants and looked about three. The other was a year younger. He had a bad stomach. A stream of thin brown liquid dripped from his backside, into the rag his mother had tied about his loins, and trickled down the backs of his legs. No one except Chintay seemed to have noticed this. Turning her eyes away from the child she faced Nishay Ghosh and held his eyes firmly with her own.

'So, Ghosh Babu,' she asked quietly, 'what do you think happened?'

Nishay Ghosh had been preparing an answer to this question for some time now. He knew it would come sooner or later.

But, face-to-face with Chintay, he lost his nerve. Somehow, he didn't know why, he was somewhat in awe of Madhai's wife. She was a woman who didn't believe in staying quietly at home like other fishwives. She was to be seen everywhere. And she had the sharpest tongue he had ever heard in a woman. She had no compunctions about letting loose a stream of filthy abuse, if crossed. She had even been known to rain blows on anyone who dared to offend her. She had argued and fought with him about delayed payment of Madhai's wages on one or two occasions. He had to be careful with her.

'What do I think? Isn't it obvious?' Nishay Ghosh, who had been shouting and raging all this while, lowered his voice. 'Your husband and his mates have run off with my boat and nets…'

'How do you know that?'

'What is there to know or not know? They weren't supposed to go to Saatmukho. Why did they?'

'One can't always stick to instructions when sailing down a river. Sometimes the current is so strong … it carries you along with it. Maybe they got caught in a whirlpool and were swept away.'

'That's a fine story. But I can't buy it. Jainal is an expert boatman. He would never be caught in a whirlpool. They had stuff worth fourteen or fifteen thousand rupees with them. They couldn't resist the temptation…'

'You have no grounds for your suspicion. They have been employed with you for years. They are not the kind of men who would steal from you.'

'Of course not.' Nishay's nose wrinkled in a sneer. 'They are models of virtue! Low-caste crooks … the lot of them. Look here, Chintay. If they return with a story of being attacked by dacoits and losing my boat and nets … they can look forward to cooling their heels in jail. I won't let them get off so easily.'

'You look here, Ghosh Babu. You have no proof to back your accusations. The river is dangerous in this season. They may be in trouble. You are their employer. You have three more boats. Why don't you send a search party in one of them and find out what has happened?'

'*A ha ha*! Excellent advice, dear lady! Your husband and his friends have dealt me this terrible blow. Made me lose thousands of rupees. And how must I react? I must spend some more money and send a search party to go looking for them! Let them be in trouble. Let them die. What do I care if the low-caste bastards have been attacked by tigers or ended up in the bellies of crocodiles?'

Palani and Zubeida burst out weeping at these words. A hush fell on the assembly. A breathless silence ensued. It lasted a few minutes, then was suddenly shattered by a cry from Chintay.

'Mind your tongue, Ghosh Babu,' she shrieked. 'Low-caste bastards indeed! Don't forget that it is these low-caste bastards that have made you rich. Whom you use to your advantage day in and day out. Of course, you don't care if they are eaten by tigers and crocodiles. Why would you? What are you but an exploiter of your fellow human beings? A man of no morals. No feelings. Shameless! Selfish to the core!'

'*Ei! Ei!* Don't you dare open your filthy mouth before me.'

'Why not? If you can call us bastards. Low caste...?'

'What shall I call you then? High-caste men and women of eminence...?'

'We are the lowest of the low. But what are you? You have money. But money hasn't made you any better than us.'

Before Nishay Ghosh could respond to this, Tagar ran forward and clasped his feet with both hands. 'Don't be angry with Didi,' she begged. 'She is distraught. She doesn't mean a word of what she is saying. We are all distraught. Won't you make a few enquiries, Babu? Whom do we have but you?'

'*Arre! Arre*!' Nishay Ghosh withdrew his feet hastily. 'Don't touch me. Go home. Let me wait for a day or two. Then I'll see what I can do.'

Chintay stepped forward and yanked Tagar by the hand. 'Stop it, Tagar,' she cried, hauling the girl to her feet. 'You will gain nothing by cringing before this devil. Come all of you…' She turned to the others. 'Let's leave this cursed place.'

'Go! Go!' Nishay Ghosh snarled. 'Get out before my men kick you out. But let me make this clear. If your husbands don't return my boat and nets, I'll make you pay. To the last paisa.'

Chintay opened her mouth to retaliate. Tagar stopped her. 'Don't utter another word, Didi,' she cried, covering it with a trembling hand. 'These aren't good people. Let's go before they do something worse to us.'

But Chintay was made of sterner stuff. Jerking Tagar's hand away from her mouth she turned slowly and stood face-to-face with Nishay Ghosh.

'Listen, Ghosh Babu,' she said, holding his small, mean eyes with her large burning ones. 'Who will make whom pay remains to be seen. But I too need to make something clear. If our husbands don't return safe and sound, we will hold *you* responsible. We won't need any police or court. We will deal with you ourselves.' She swept out of the room, leaving Nishay Ghosh gaping at her.

Outside, the scudding clouds had vanished. The sky hung above the women's heads, a blue-black sheet, out of which thousands of stars winked and glimmered. A wasted moon threw a dull haze across it. Leaving the bazar behind, they stopped at the turn of the road that led to the jetty and stared at one another. They had been quite voluble all this while but now, when the time had come to part ways, all tongues were stilled.

'Palani lives in Nikarighata.' Chintay broke the silence. 'She'll reach home in an hour. But what will you two do?' She turned to Zubeida and Tagar who lived in Henrhodanga.

'It will take us three hours to reach the village,' Tagar replied worriedly. 'We could have done it if we were by ourselves. The trouble is, I have two midgets with me and Zubeida has one. They will never be able to walk all the way. Look, they're falling asleep already. We will stay in Palani's house tonight.'

'That's a good idea,' Chintay said, 'but getting back home will not solve our problem. We will have to think about what to do next.'

'What can we do?'

'Let's wait for three days. If our men come back by then ... well and good. If not, we will have to plan our next move. I'll tell you what. Today is Tuesday. Come to my house on Saturday morning. We will put our heads together and figure out the way forward. You will find my house easily enough. Just take my name. Everyone in Sonakhali knows where I live.'

Tagar and Zubeida nodded. Palani broke into a fresh spasm of tears. 'What will become of us, Didi?' she asked between sobs.

'Don't weep, sister. We're in this together. We will bring Nishay Ghosh to his knees.'

*

Chintay came home in a daze. In the boat, on her way across the river, she had sat huddled beside the prow not speaking a word. Her fellow travellers had tried to make conversation; had asked questions. But nothing had registered. She hadn't heard or uttered a word.

Chintay paid the boatman and stepped out on the bank at Sonakhali. The tide being high, she climbed up the dyke easily. She walked home, her steps tottering as though she were drunk. Her mind was in a whirl. Where was Madhai and what had happened to him? Had he and his companions sold the boat and nets as Nishay Ghosh suspected and were, even now, making merry with the money? No, she didn't think so. She was sure they were in some sort of trouble. But what could she do about it? To whom could she turn? If she borrowed a boat and went sailing down the Matla, she might glean some information from the villages along the banks. But how could she, a lone woman, undertake such a venture? She could, of course, take Palani and the others with her. They had talked about it, already, in a desultory fashion. Zubeida could do the steering and the others take turns at the oars. But they had four children between them. Where would they leave the little ones? Besides, the moment the animals who went by the name of *men* saw four women without a male escort, they would pounce on them and tear them to bits. The dangers of snakes and wild animals prowling in the woods along the river would be nothing in comparison.

Tagar, Zubeida and Palani came to Chintay's house, somewhat late, on Saturday morning. They had left the children in the care of sisters and aunts for who knew what lay in store for them the rest of the day? They would have to run here and there talking to boatmen and fishermen and make fresh enquiries at Nishay Ghosh's warehouse. They might even have to file a Missing Persons' Report at the local thana. All this activity would be impossible with children clinging to their sari ends.

Chintay had cooked a good meal that morning. Rice, dal, a rich phyansa fish curry and another of bhola, sharp and spicy, with mustard and chillies. She hadn't done any cooking since

Madhai went missing, managing to survive on muri and bread. She had spent all her time, looking for her husband, in Canning and the surrounding villages. Moulay, Boulay, Gosaba, Chunokhali ... even as far as Taldi, deep in the Sundarbans, where men often went to fish in the rivers, to cut wood and take down hives dripping with honey. No one had seen them. But despite her disappointment a tiny flame of hope flickered in her breast. No reports of a boat wreck or drowning had come either. Nor of maulings by tigers. Which meant that Madhai and his companions were alive. It was possible that their boat had been sucked into a whirlpool then swept away by strong currents to a place so far off that it would take them a week, or even more, to return to Sonakhali.

After lunch the women sat on a mat in the yard and Chintay shared all this information and more. Nishay Ghosh had carried out his threat of lodging an FIR with the local thana. He had come to Chintay's house, yesterday evening, accompanied by a policeman with a summons. He had told her that if the boat and nets were not returned within a week, Chintay's house would be sealed and all her household goods confiscated. Not that Chintay's household goods amounted to much. The price they fetched would by no means cover Nishay's loss. But, from what she had heard, Nishay had another, more devious, plan in mind. He meant to drive her and the other women away from their huts and sell the land on which they stood.

Palani was a timid, soft-natured girl. All she had done the last three days was weep till her eyes were red and swollen. Now, after hearing Chintay's account, the tears poured down her cheeks in streams. Zubeida rose to console her but the tougher Tagar averted her gaze from the weeping girl. Her eyes were fixed on the hog plum tree where a flock of wild parrots were flitting in and out of the branches with swift flashes of jewel-green wings. Her brow was furrowed as though in deep thought.

'You are very quiet, Tagar?' Chintay said. 'What's on your mind?'

Tagar stood up with a sudden movement. Throwing herself at Chintay's feet, she answered in a trembling voice, 'We've done something very wrong, Didi. We didn't tell you because…'

Chintay glanced at the three faces, one by one. Fear, guilt and pain were stamped on each.

'Why do you say that?' she asked surprised. 'What have you done?'

'The three of us met Nishay Ghosh yesterday. We pleaded with him…'

'What!' Chintay cried out, shocked. 'And then?'

'He's a devil incarnate, Didi. Our tears and pleas would have melted a stone. But his heart is harder. He kept repeating his threat. If his boat and nets were not returned, he would drive us out of our huts. But…' Tagar hesitated and added, a little shamefacedly, 'he gave us an option.'

'What option?'

'He asked us to work in his warehouse. If we agreed he would give us two meals a day and a salary out of which he would deduct a small amount every month till he made up the money he had lost. But the working hours would be long. From morning till late at night.'

'The warehouse is closed from noon till dusk. What work will you do, then, and where?'

'That he didn't say. But he…'

'O lo, O Mukhpurhi!' Chintay gave a snort of laughter. 'Are you a complete idiot? Or have you just dropped from your mother's womb? Don't you realize that Nishay Ghosh doesn't

want your work? He wants *you*. He's lusting after your young bodies. He was always a dirty womanizer but he's become worse after his wife died. There's a tiny room just behind the warehouse where he sleeps with a different woman every night. Sometimes he turns it into a brothel and allows other men in. He makes money that way.'

'*O Ma go*!' The three faces before her turned pale with horror. 'We had no idea…'

'Of course, you didn't. You don't live here. But I…' Chintay didn't complete her sentence. She turned her face away. There was a strange look in her eyes. 'I know that villain through and through,' she said after a while. 'He tried to trap me too. He came to my house and promised to treat me like a queen if I agreed to sleep with him. This was right in the beginning when my man first started working for him. He threatened to sack him if I didn't agree…'

'Then?'

'Then!' Chintay burst into a peal of laughter. 'I chased him out with my broomstick. I threatened to tell everyone. Cowardly dog that he is, he ran away with his tail between his legs.' She was quiet for a few moments, then went on in a faraway voice, 'Our lives, low-caste people's lives, are bitter. Filled with salt. Saltier than the salt streams that flow through the length and breadth of the fen in which we live. Look your hardest into them … you won't find a tinge of honey. We live in constant fear. Of tigers on the ground and crocodiles in the water. We have to struggle, just to survive, all the time. All the time. Every moment of the day. And even worse than the beasts are the moneylenders. No matter how hard we try to avoid them, they manage to get us into their clutches.'

'What will become of us?' Tagar muttered worriedly. 'Our husbands show no sign of returning. If Nishay Ghosh carries out his threat and throws us out, where will we go? We have small children…'

'That's what I've been pondering over these last three days. Listen, sisters. Weeping and cringing before that devil will get us nowhere. We will have to fight.'

'Fight! How can we do that?'

'There is a way. Haven't you seen men and women walking in processions? Carrying banners and shouting *"Fight! Fight! Fight! We must fight to live!"* I've seen so many.'

'But how … how?' Three puzzled faces were turned to Chintay's.

'*Arre*! Don't you realize that our fight has begun already? Have I been sitting idle these three days? I've gone from door to door. I've talked to all the men who work for Nishay Ghosh. I told them that Madhai and the others are clearly in some trouble and it is the master's duty to send search parties and bring them home. Instead, he has set the police on us and is threatening to evict us. Is such behaviour to be tolerated? "We live precarious lives," I said. "We are stalked by danger all the time. What has happened to my man today, can happen to you tomorrow. We must band together against that scoundrel if we wish to survive."'

'And then?'

'They hesitated a bit, in the beginning, but agreed in the end. They have stopped work, as a mark of protest, and Nishay's boats have been lying idle since then. Nishay Ghosh is in a fix. He's been running around like a mad dog. Now to the police; now to his workers begging them to return.'

'Really, Didi!' The three faces brightened visibly. 'Good that he has been taught a lesson.'

'He hasn't got his full dues yet. We will tighten the screw. I have an idea. Stay in my house tonight and let's make a plan. We will have to strike swiftly. In the next couple of days.'

'Please do something quickly, Didi.' Palani let out a loud sob. 'My man hasn't come home for five days now. I feel so helpless without him. I have two babies. How will I fend for them? *O Ma go!*'

Zubeida had been silent all this while. She was a quiet, repressed girl, not given to showing her feelings. But now she sat up with a jerk and spoke with a strange urgency in her voice. 'Why are we wasting our time sitting here? We should go looking for our husbands. We will look everywhere, in every possible and impossible place. We will search far and near, high and low. We will scour every nook and cranny. Find them we must. But let's get one thing clear. No one will help us. Not Nishay Ghosh. Not the other fisher folk. And certainly not the police.' She took a deep breath and went on, 'Men look down on us. They scorn us as weak and helpless. Let's show them that we aren't what they think. We can do everything they can. We are four women together. We will find our men by ourselves. Never fear.'

Chintay put her arms around Zubeida and drew her to her bosom. This was the response she had craved for. These were the words she had wanted to hear. Zubeida's thoughts were in exact consonance with hers. She was so moved … her limbs trembled with an unknown emotion. Tears gushed out of her eyes and ran down her cheeks. Were they tears of joy? Or of sorrow? She didn't know…

*

The light of evening has dimmed. Dusk has given way to night. On the vast vault above, black as a buffalo's belly, stars twinkle like flowers of fire. On this night, the penultimate night of the cycle of the waning moon, the sky is as clear as glass…

Four women can be seen walking on the dyke along the river. Their heads, arms and hips are laden with sacks and bundles, pots and pans, baskets and coils of rope. Chintay is leading the way and the other three are following her with slow, measured steps.

The bazar is deserted. So is the jetty. The men are all in Canning. They've gone to see the jatra which is being performed by a reputed troupe. There being no moon tonight, the tide will come in late. After midnight. Boats will set sail only when the tide is full. Boatmen and fishermen of the salt fens of Sundarbans have time, till then, to enjoy themselves.

The four women walk slowly. Cautiously. As though afraid of their own shadows. In the dim light of glow-worms, flickering from trees and bushes, they look like ghosts of fishwives, long dead and gone. Moving silhouettes. Devoid of colour and sound.

Now, reaching a fork in the road, the figures come to life. The rail station and bazar are to their right. But they take the left. They walk past a number of trees and bushes till they reach a tube well. Chintay whispers something. Tagar and Zubeida fill two large pots with water. They start walking again…

A cold breeze starts to blow from the river that stretches, vast and formidable, just ahead of them. A shiver ripples through the group. 'O Chintay Didi!' Tagar whispers fearfully. 'What place is this? You said we would rent a boat from the ghat and go looking for our husbands.'

'Look ahead of you. What do you see?'

'I see three boats lined along the bank. But where are the…?'

'They are Nishay's boats. We will take one of them.'

'Na na, Didi. We don't want to have *anything* to do with Nishay Ghosh again!'

'Why not? Two boats and nets have been stolen from him. A third will disappear. Simple.'

'What if someone sees us?'

'No one will see us. I have made enquiries. Everyone is in Canning enjoying the jatra. Mark my words. No one will return before dawn.'

'*O Ma go!* What will happen to my little ones?' Palani exclaimed suddenly and burst into loud sobs.

'*What will happen to my little ones*?' Chintay mimicked the girl cruelly. 'They will remain where they are until we return. Just that. And if we don't return, they will be taken care of. Your sisters and aunts won't throw them out on the streets, will they? Come, let's go.'

But Palani stood where she was and continued to weep.

'Stop your sniffles, you fool!' Chintay gritted her teeth at the girl. 'Make up your mind. Do you want your children or your husband? You needn't come with us. No one is forcing you. Go back.'

'Stop it, Palani,' Zubeida hissed a warning. 'Don't make a scene. Let's go ahead with what we decided to do. Looking behind will only weaken our resolve.'

The space between the bank and the river had turned into a quagmire. The women had a long way to walk before they reached Nishay Ghosh's boats. It was a most difficult crossing. At places they sank knee deep in the mud left by the ebbing waters. The ends of their saris got entangled in thorn bushes and tufts of tussock grass. But they pushed on and on, straining against the cold night wind, till they came to the first boat. Heaving a sigh of relief, they laid down their burdens. Sacks of rice and dal, jars of oil, potatoes, salt, spices and kerosene. Enough to supply them with food for a week or so. They had made up their minds. They would scour all the banks and villages in the Sundarbans till they found their husbands. They wouldn't return without them. What would be the point of returning anyway? Only to fall into the mouths of sharks and crocodiles like Nishay Ghosh? It was far better to be swept away by the waters. Carried on by swift currents, past forest and marshland, from the Matla to other bigger rivers. Till they reached…?

Zubeida cut the rope that tied the first boat to a tree with a knife she carried at her waist and the four women started pushing it down the wet and slippery slope. But just before they reached the river, Chintay lifted a hand and stopped them. 'Wait,' she said. 'There's something I need to do first.' Picking up the tin of kerosene, she turned and started walking in the direction of the bank from where they had come. The others stared in wonder at her strong healthy form, bent against the wind, struggling against mud, slush and slime.

Tagar, Zubeida and Palani sat in the well of the boat for what seemed hours. They had lost count of time. There was a change in the air. It was getting darker and colder every moment and a fine mist was wrapping them in its folds. Sky and river had merged into a vault of inky black studded with pinpoints of light from a few feeble stars glimmering between patches of cloud. They were looking on, it seemed to the women, with wonder at the sight of three fishwives sitting in a boat at dead of night. It was so dark they could barely see each other. Gusts of cold damp wind, blowing from the river, made their teeth chatter. Their hearts went numb with fear. What had happened to Chintay? Had she trapped them in this dangerous situation only to abandon them? Or had she been caught by Nishay Ghosh's men and was, even now, in his custody.

Suddenly the silence of the night was broken. A flock of night birds flew above their heads, flapping their wings in terror. A pack of wild dogs started howling. And with them could be heard shouts from human voices. The women rose to their feet. The bazar ahead of them was blazing with light, as though lit with a thousand torches.

And now a shadow came creeping down the bank. Silhouetted against a sky as bright as day, it swung this way and that winding its way down the slippery slope till it reached the boat. It was Chintay. She was covered with mud from head to foot. Tangled hair streamed down her back. The end of her sari flew in the wind as she ran panting towards the group. 'Let's go,' she said. 'Get out of the boat and push it into the water. Be quick. There's no time to lose.'

'What light is that?' the three women cried out in frightened voices.

'That?' Chintay grinned and hissed into their ears. 'That's Nishay's warehouse. It's burning to ashes.'

The True Life Story of Uli-Buli's Mother

Mahasweta Devi

In the station area and the bazaar adjoining it, I am known as Uli-Buli'r Ma. But, believe me, if I see Uli and Buli today I won't recognize them. I haven't seen them for twenty-four years. A span of twelve years makes a yuga. So, two yugas have gone by without my eyes catching a glimpse of my twin girls. They were only a year old when it happened…

'Shame on you!' my husband used to say. 'First one girl, then another, and now two together! I'll find myself another wife.'

'Do that,' I would weep and plead. 'But don't drive me away. I'll move out of the house and live in the cowshed with the bull calf.'

'*I'll live in the cowshed with the bull calf!* What will you eat?'

'I work in five houses even now, cleaning cowsheds and making dung cakes. I'll feed myself.'

Ma re! Those days were different. The bridge in Kasba was built many years later. Our village had no railway station. I would get off at Dhamuya and walk two miles through mud and slime.

Father's house? *Hee Hee Hee*. Does a girl have a father's house after she's wed? *Ma re!* In homes like yours there are only one or two children. Parents love you and take care of you even after you're wed. The old lady I call Didma, you know the one who lives in that double-storeyed house? Well, she's selling it and going to American to live with her granddaughter. What did you say? It isn't American … it's some other place? Well, I don't know about that. But once she gave me a piece of soap as small as a matchbox. What a wonderful scent it had! When I bathed at the roadside tap, the air would smell of roses. No wonder Didma, even in her old age, looks so young!

Anyway, my husband got married. You know what happened next? *O Ma! O Ma!* He told me he was moving in with his in-laws. They didn't have a son. They wanted a *ghar jamai*. What's more, he was selling off all his property in the village. Cruel! Cruel!

I summoned up all my courage and approached the village elders. 'No land. No roof above my head,' I wept. 'Where will I live? I have four daughters…'

'It was a wrong thing to do!' Janardan's father shook his white head. 'One ten, one nine and the other two … only a year old! Where will the poor woman go?'

'Why does she give birth *only* to girls?' Janardan hollered. 'I've heard Dada say that she went prancing to the pond anytime she felt like it. She would eat mussel *chachharhi* on Saturdays! Won't evil spirits enter such a woman's body and spoil her womb?'

'Shut your mouth, sister-fucker!' the father snarled. 'Always judging others! Don't I know you? Dirty land grabber!'

Suddenly my husband's cousin Janak appeared on the scene. He had been caught in a train dacoity and just been released from prison. 'Will I let anyone drive out my pure and chaste Boudi from her home and stand idly by?' he thundered in his dacoit's voice. 'Who's buying the property?

'Janardan...'

'Oh! Really? I'll slash their throats. Dada's first and then this scoundrel's. Boudi will be widowed. So what? I'll be hanged. Very good. But I won't allow a woman to be hurt.'

Silence. Everyone feared Janak. There was no panchayat in those days. Twelve greybeards sat with long faces and discussed the matter. The decision reached was that husbands would be found for the two older girls. And they were. One bridegroom needed a second wife and the other a third. Everything was sold. The house and land, the bull calf, my nose stud and ear-rings...

A few days after the girls left for their husbands' homes, havoc broke loose. Such a storm! *Ma re!* Such rain, thunder and lightning! Floods in the month of Bhadra! Can you believe it? People from all the surrounding villages had to leave and come to the city. I did too. We took shelter wherever we could find. In the station platform, under sheds in Kumor Parha, on verandas of rich men's houses. There were so many people with me in that double-storeyed house, I've lost count. I would beg during the day and sleep under the porch at night. And it was from there that my Uli and Buli were stolen...

The rain just wouldn't stop. There was a pond in Kumor Parha where I used to bathe. I didn't know my way about the streets very well those days. Well, it was just before Durga Puja ... Ma Durga must have travelled by boat all the way from Kailash that year. They used to give us khichurhi in the ashram. They even gave clothes sometimes. I'll be lying if I denied it. There was an old woman in Magarhaat who warned me. 'Be careful daughter,' she said, 'Kolkata is full of thieves and dacoits...'

Well, that's what happened. Both my girls were stolen. Buli had a fair skin. Uli was dark. Later, much later, I heard that baby girls get kidnapped in the city. Their arms and legs are broken and they're turned into beggars. *Ma re!* How I wept and beat my breast! You see that paan shop? There was a shop selling bread next to it. I used to creep under the shed and weep and weep and weep.

No, I never thought of going back to the village. Why would I? No land, no house, no one I could call my own! You see that ashram over there? They used to give me muri and batasha. I used to sweep and swab the yard with cow-dung.

'Child!' Manager babu said to me, 'you are young. Why don't you work?'

'Who'll give me work, Baba?'

'You called me Baba!'

'My own father got me married and…'

'No husband?'

'Drove me out long ago. In the year of the great flood, I came to…'

'Will you work in my house? The mistress is bedridden. Pains all over her body. Stay with us, eat well. I'll give you ten rupees a month.'

'His wife is a suspicious woman,' the boy in the paan shop whispered in my ear. 'Maids don't stick in his house.'

Manager babu gave me two red saris. Offerings from devotees. I started working. Ginni Ma troubled me at first. But I didn't give up. I called her Ma. Her husband Baba. I pressed her feet. I massaged her limbs with Kobreji oil. At night I slept on the floor in her room. Ginni Ma took to me. 'Buy her plastic bangles from the pavement stall,' she told the other maid. 'Blouse and petticoat I'll give her myself.'

I stayed with them for three years. A son had been born to

them. He died of some illness, I don't know what, at the age of seven. They loved hearing the sound of Ma and Baba from my lips. But *Ma re!* Wherever you go your fate follows you. I had changed in those three years. I was happy. Your sorrows vanish when you have rice in your belly, clothes on your body and oil to cool your head.

Lightning struck. Baba's heart failed and he died. No warning. What a time that was *Ma re!* What a time! I sobbing and screaming! Ma weeping and beating her breast! Someone informed them in the ashram. They came and took the body away. It was then that I heard Baba had willed everything he had to the ashram. His house, his money, the care of his wife.

'The girl looks after me,' Ginni Ma said to them. 'I would be dead without her. I want to keep her on.'

'There are many women in the ashram,' they replied. 'But we will see … we will see.'

There were two other girls working in the house. 'Come with me,' one said, 'I'll find you work. Stay in my room in Kumor Parha and share the rent. Thirty rupees.'

I went. *Ma re!* A tiny slip of a room! Thirty rupees rent! I found work in two houses. With Didma and the Marwaris who live in the big four-storeyed house.

Now? *Now?* Don't you know? Everyone knows. Why don't you?

'What don't I know?'

You don't need to know anything. Why do you ask so many questions? You give me food. True. You give me clothes. But how can you not know that Uli-Bulis are sold in the hospital? That when I heard that, I rushed to buy them back?

'No child. I didn't know. I truly didn't.'

*

It was Shaili who saved me. 'Why do waste your time talking to her?' she scolded. 'You gave her food. Very good. But after that you should have sent her away. Don't you know that she spews this rubbish before everyone she can find?'

Uli-Buli's mother was unfazed. She cleaned the space where she had eaten the meal I had given her with expert hands, packed her bowl and thala in her rag bundle, and made her way to the gate. I watched her as she walked away.

'Everyone knows her story,' Shaili said.

'Did she really go to the hospital?'

'She did. "I've come to buy my Uli-Buli," she said. "Give them to me." She got a good beating.'

'When did this happen?'

'Four years ago.'

'Does she know you?'

'She used to live in Kumor Parha at one time. I knew her then.'

'Where does she live now?'

'Under the bridge. She sleeps in a tiny space between two shops. *Uli-Buli, Uli-Buli* ... she rambles all the time! She came here after she was beaten up at the hospital.'

'I didn't know...'

'You were away at that time. That's why. I give her food from time to time.'

'Clothes? She told me I give her clothes.'

'I give her my old saris and tell her they are from you.'

'Her daughters would have been twenty-four years old today ... wouldn't they?'

'She doesn't understand that. She searches her one-year-olds. She thinks she will find them someday.'

'Did she work at one time?'

'She did. But she has been on the streets after she left Kumor Parha.'

'It's good that she comes to you.'

'The people in the street mock her, "Look," they cry out, "look, look! There's your Uli-Buli." Poor mad creature! She'll die any day. But people have no pity.'

'What does she say?'

'She howls and beats her breast. Swears and curses. Rushes at them. She looks the way she does but she's really quite young.'

I believed Shaili. Perhaps all women with a life story like Uli-Buli's mother look like her.

Nalini's Story

Mahasweta Devi

Morning

As on all other days, Nalini had risen at dawn, done her chores and taken a bath. She had worn a flimsy yellow sari bought from the footpath last year with her Durga Puja tips. 'This is called synthetic garad, Mashi,' the seller had told her. Synthetic garad was fine. But after bringing it home she noticed a few holes in the anchal. There was no question of taking it back. So now she had turned it into her puja sari. She lit the lamp before the image of Kali every morning and burned some incense sticks.

Her worthy grandson had tried his hand at many trades but failed every time, his only capital being a stentorian voice and an infinite capacity to roam under the hottest of suns. On the advice of the community elder, Nalini had sent him out to sell incense. This was one business that couldn't fail, he had assured her. One packet cost four rupees. But if you bought three packets you paid ten.

But that failed too. So, now, Nalini used the leftover stock of incense for her morning puja. After paying her obeisance to the image of Ma Kali, she changed into an everyday sari, lit the stove and cooked a one-pot meal for her grandson who was still asleep. He slept all the time. It wasn't that he didn't know he was twenty years old and that he had failed in his duty to his old grandmother. He often expressed his regret. But Nalini was not impressed 'Stop spewing that old garbage over and over again,' she would retort.

'I spew old garbage?'

'What else? Your father did the same in his time. Everyone has done their duty by me! Now it's your turn. Stop worrying about me. Do what you will but always remember what I've taught you. Don't take the wrong path. Don't turn to evil ways. One thing is clear though. There'll be no one to feed you after I'm gone. Keep that in mind. When you're married and have children…'

'Baba got married too.'

'Yes. He did.'

'He dumped me on you and left. He is involved in some shady business these days. He doesn't lift a finger for me. How can he? With three other children?'

'Forget your father. He kicked me out of his life and went away years ago…'

'He wants to come back…'

'I know. He wants our two rooms and the yard. He doesn't know that I made a will long ago and left them to you.'

'As if I'll stay here after you're gone!'

'Stay wherever you like when the time comes. But for now, make haste and go to the market. Buy potatoes and kanthal seeds. And flowers for my puja.'

'Gobindo Jetha says…'

'I know what he says. He smuggles stuff from Bangladesh and sells it here. He wants you as a helper. But I won't let you join him. Boys die of gunshots at the border every other day.'

Nalini eats a bowl of leftover rice as she talks. Then packing a paan and a wad of tobacco in her mouth, she wears her rubber chappals and leaves the house. She'll walk to the station, and catch the train to Jadavpur. From there, she'll take a rickshaw to Golf Green. She works here till twelve. Boudidi leaves for her office early in the morning, Dada at noon. The little girl takes the school bus at nine and returns at three.

Nalini works diligently all morning. She cleans the rooms, washes the clothes, and fills big bottles with filtered water. There is a water filter in every house these days. The woman who does the cooking comes at twelve thirty. Dada tells her what to cook in Bangla mixed with English. Nalini marvels at how trusting Dada and Boudidi are. They've given them both keys to the house. They can come in and go out as they please. Nalini is paid six hundred rupees. And Boudidi has told her to have a meal before she starts her work. Rice, ruti … whatever she wants. Nalini likes her though she feels uncomfortable addressing a woman with bobbed hair, wearing pants and top, as Boudidi.

The cook Sumila left her husband years ago and lives with a shopkeeper in Bikramgarh. *Au! Au! Au!* What a shameless creature! She eats everything. Fish, meat, chicken … she gobbles it all. 'You're so silly, Mashi,' she tells Nalini, 'You're allowed to eat anything you like. Eat!'

'You eat.'

Boudidi has bought Sumila an apron. She comes to work all decked up in colourful saris and shiny blouses. She sits for a while in Boudidi's air-conditioned room and rests, then switches on the radio and listens to music as she cooks. She washes her hands with Boudidi's fragrant soap before she leaves. All her work is done in a haphazard manner. Shameless woman! As old as the hills and dresses like a girl! Foreign soap! Fair and Lovely! Her daughter is exactly like her. *Oof!*

Sumila gets eight hundred rupees.

After finishing her chores Nalini rests for a while under a tree. At one o'clock, she reports for duty in her next house, a flat on the third floor of a six-storeyed mansion. A mother and daughter live here. Didi's husband lives in America. He has a big business there, a house and a car. He had been living with a Pakistani woman for a number of years but hadn't married her. Things have changed now. Husband and wife are reconciled. That's why Didi has brought her daughter back from her boarding school. They will leave for America in a few months.

But what about the mother? Ginni Ma says she will leave the house to whoever takes care of her. Didi protests. Fights break out between them every day. Nalini works here till dusk. She keeps everything ready for the evening meal, kneads the dough, washes Ginni Ma's clothes and irons them. The old lady has an attendant. But it is Nalini who must powder her body, comb her wispy white hair and plait it. Ginni Ma has money of her own. She gets a pension from the government. She pays Nalini seven hundred rupees. She can't do without her.

Nalini was dusting her room and listening to her chatter when Sumila burst in. 'Mashi! O Mashi!' she cried. 'Listen, listen…'

'What's the matter, Sumila?'

'Do you know someone called Gobindo Mandal?'

'We live in the same parha.'

'He telephoned Dada in the office and told him that your husband is dead. He died in Bangladesh. Gobindo Mandal told Dada to send you home at once.'

'Nalini's husband!' Ginni Ma exclaimed.

'You heard me, Dida.'

'He died in Bangladesh?'

'So … so he never left the village?' Nalini cried out in a bewildered voice. 'I'd better go at once, Ma. My heart is beating like a drum. Who knows what all I'll need to do.'

'Gobindo Mandal will tell you.'

'Will you come with me to the station, Sumila? I'll take a rickshaw.'

'Let's hurry. I have a lot of cooking left. *Baap re!* How much food these rich people eat! Green peas and cauliflower in summer. Jhinge and patol in winter. Come, come. Quick.'

The old lady was enjoying the conversation. There was an eager look on her face. But Nalini's head was swimming. Her legs were tottering.

'I'm going, Ma.'

'Don't touch my feet, child. You need to bathe first.'

'Only bathe!' Sumila exclaimed. 'Mashi is from the bauri caste. There'll be many other rites.'

Nalini felt as though a hostile crowd was closing in on her. Assaulting her.

'Make haste, Mashi.' Sumila quickened her steps. 'You won't be able to come for some days now. Shall I tell Boudidi?'

'Na na. Let me go home first. Let me see…'

'Hai! Hai! You set out in the morning with no idea at all of what had happened. And suddenly this news…'

Nalini nodded. Her hairline had receded over the years and revealed a dome of a forehead. A streak of sindoor on her bald head, an iron hoop on her left wrist and a pair of plastic bangles proclaimed her marital status. Though small and slight, it was obvious that her body was tough and resilient.

She works hard the whole day and returns at dusk. She changes her sari and splashes some water on her face and neck. Washes her hands. Then she sits in the doorway and fans herself with her anchal. She chats with her neighbours for a while. Then she gets up and examines what her grandson has brought from the bazaar. Though fish is cheap in Canning, they can afford to buy it only once in a while. Their daily fare is ruti and pumpkin curry. Sometimes she gives the boy a lump of gur as a special treat. He curses his father with every mouthful. 'What sort of man is he? Eats fish and crabs with every meal but doesn't once think of us.'

'Gobindo says he'll get you a job in his wheat mill. Once you have a steady job our troubles will be over.'

'He will? Really?'

'Of course he will. Didn't I give him two hundred rupees when he started his business?'

Years go by. Hope dwindles. The boy is twelve years old when he fails in Class Seven. He stops going to school and spends his time hanging around the bazaar. He sells vegetables for Gobindo Mandal sometimes, and gets four annas per rupee out of the profits. In winter he peddles Joy Bangla sweaters, caps, pants, frocks and vests in the streets of Kolkata. Nalini feels sorry for him. She decides to ask Dada for a loan of two hundred rupees this Puja. She will buy him a nice shirt, pants and vest…

But this one bit of news wipes away Nalini's afternoon and evening and turns the day into the darkest of nights.

Dusk to Evening

She sees her daughter-in-law even before she enters the house. A large flabby woman of thirty-five standing in the middle of a group of women, blabbering excitedly. At the sight of Nalini all fall silent.

'Gobindo! O Gobindo! Mashi has arrived.'

Gobindo comes forward. 'Has Dada given you the news?'

'He has.'

'Come into the house. Your son was informed. He is here already.'

'Let me have some water first and rest for a while.'

'You'd better hurry,' Gobindo says in a patronizing voice. As though he was in charge. As though the responsibility for handling the matter rested solely on his shoulders. 'There's no time to lose. Your husband died twenty-three days ago.'

'He died at home?'

'No. He was taken to the hospital. Poor man! He suffered for months before he died.'

'Was it in sixty-four that I came here? Or sixty-five?'

'How does that matter? It was more than forty years ago.'

'I was twenty-five. My son was seven. In all these years he didn't enquire after our welfare even once. I was his wife after all. I had borne him a son. Yet he abandoned us...'

'Let bygones be bygones. The fact is that you've been widowed. Your husband died twenty-three days ago and...'

'I came in nineteen sixty-five.' Nalini's voice sounded faraway. 'I came with your sister. The government gave us refuge. But you brought us here...'

'Why rake up the past? It's the present that matters. I've made enquiries about the funeral rites mandatory for a widow of your caste. Suraj, the temple priest, explained them in detail. You must take a bath and wear a thaan. That's the first thing. Then...'

'Thaan?' A loud exclamation came hurtling through the air. It was Mukundo's mother's voice. Mukundo was Gobindo's tenant and everyone called her Mukundo'r Ma. 'Since when have bauri widows started wearing thaans? Are you placing us on the same level as Brahmin and Kayastha women?'

A clamour of voices rose in the air. Some supporting Mukundo'r Ma. Others not.

'Very well then. Let me buy a couple of black-bordered dhutis,' Gobindo offered.

'What else? What else have you thought up in that scheming brain of yours?'

The younger generation had become quite confrontational. The old lessons in meekness and obedience were not working these days. '*Thaan porbe!*' a girl from the crowd shouted. 'Why should she wear a thaan, pray? Her man hasn't even looked at her for forty years. And now, just because he's dead, she must wear a thaan all her life!'

Another clamour of voices.

'Mashi's son is here,' Gobindo said hurriedly. 'Let's leave the decision to him.'

'Where's he?' Nalini spoke up for the first time. 'I haven't seen him for years. His wife died giving birth. And what did he do? He dumped his new-born son on me and disappeared. Married again and started another family. Has he ever bothered to find out how we live or sent me a single rupee?'

'But, Mashi,' Gobindo's strident voice became conciliatory, 'he is the head of the family now. We can't proceed without discussing the details with him.'

'What details?'

'Well, firstly you must take a bath, wash away your sindoor and discard your iron hoop. Next you must throw out all the food from your kitchen and wash the vessels. Then…'

'Her grandson has washed the vessels and cleaned the house,' Mukundo'r Ma interrupted in a voice as menacing as a clap of thunder. 'All that's left is to send for the priest and make an offering of til and tulsi. What more do you expect from a poor woman like her? An elaborate daan sagar? Not only is she forced to work at the age of sixty-four, she has a grandson hanging from her neck. There's no need for further talk.'

At this point Nalini's worthy son leaps into the fray. 'Gobindo dada and I have consulted the priest and been instructed in the scriptural rulings,' he says pompously. 'The dead man is Ma's husband. Whether he lived with her or not is immaterial. She has to carry out the proper rites. A period of penance before the sraddha followed by a meal for the entire clan. If she can't afford rice and fish curry, she may feed them curd and chirey.'

'Well said,' the old woman glared at him, 'and who'll pay for it? You?'

'Gobindo dada will give her the money.'

'Of course he will. In return he'll grab her house and make you join his dirty business.'

'Her soul will burn in hell if the rites are not conducted properly.'

'O *Ma go*! Such a worthy son! So concerned for his mother's soul!'

'It's not only she who will suffer. The curse will fall upon me too. And my children. I don't see the problem. Gobindo dada will give the money as a loan. She can return it later. But Ma isn't prepared to listen…'

In the midst of all this squabbling Nalini cried out suddenly, 'Bubi! Where's Bubi?'

'Here I am, Thakma.'

'Take me into the house. I feel ill. My limbs are trembling.'

'Here, hold my hand,' Mukundo'r Ma said, then turning to Gobindo she added, 'I am your tenant, Gobindo. You're my landlord. And you've dealt with me most cruelly. You forced my son and grandson to join your business. But you'd better not play the same dirty trick on Nalini. She has pulled the yoke for years and years. And she's still doing so. She lives from hand to mouth. Why should she conduct a sraddha on the same scale as Brahmin and Kayastha widows? That, too, for an absentee husband? Nalini's son is no better than an animal. And her grandson is a burden on her. You'd better get the sraddha over as quickly and cheaply as possible.'

'However hard I try the cost will come to a couple of thousands. It's impossible to go below this.'

'Two thousand?' Nalini's head started spinning. Her body gave way. Her grandson picked her up in his arms and took her into the house. 'Lay her on the floor,' Mukundo'r Ma told him. 'Let her catch her breath. There's no need to worry. I'll get everything done. Leave the room now.'

Nalini's heart flutters. Her eyes close in weariness.

Night

Nalini's senses were numbed. She was floating in a dark void. A sprinkle of water on her face made her open her eyes.

'Would you like to drink some water, Thakma?' her grandson's voice came buzzing into her ears.

'Yes, yes, give her some water first, then something to eat. I've soaked khoi and batasha.'

Nalini stared at the ceiling. She had changed the straw only a few months earlier. 'I'd like to go outside,' she muttered. She rose slowly. Her body felt as light as air. Mukundo'r Ma led her into the tiny strip of a yard surrounded by a nettle hedge. 'Don't listen to a word they say,' she whispered. 'That Gobindo and your son are in cahoots.'

'I know that, Didi.'

Nalini drinks some water, eats some khoi and batasha and lies down again. 'I feel sleepy, Didi,' she murmurs.

'Sleep in peace. There's no one in the house. Your son has gone with Gobindo.'

'Of course he has. He's his father's son after all.'

'Your grandson loves you.'

'He can't stick to a job…'

'They are all the same. Look at my son. Years and years at the border. Who knows what he does there. Doesn't send me a paisa.'

'It's all Gobindo's doing. He catches them young and wedges them to his wheel. Squeezes the life out of them. And when they are reduced to fibre, he chucks them out.'

'But when Sudhir Mandal died at the border, Gobindo gave his wife two thousand rupees.' The old woman yawns and shuts her eyes. She falls asleep. But Nalini can't sleep. She looks out of the open window. *A widow*, she rolls the word over her tongue, *but did I ever have a husband?*

Srimati Nalini. Hindu female. Father: Late Nafarchandra Das. Husband: Abodh Das. Residence: Bonpara, Khadimpur. Age: 25.

This was what Gobindo's father had written in his big red book. He had brought his family to India in 1952 and Nalini had come with her seven-year-old son in 1965. Gobindo's father had settled them here. This was all wasteland at that time. Gradually it got filled up with refugees.

Nalini had brought her silver waistband, gold armlets and nose-ring without telling her husband. She had sold them and built her two rooms with the money. The documents were obtained much later.

Married at the age of eleven she had come to her husband's home at seventeen. There was a co-wife in the house and she was the mistress. The kitchen was under her control. There was a clear division of work. Nalini ground the spices, cleaned and cut fish, chopped vegetables, scoured vessels and washed clothes at the river ghat. The co-wife stirred the ladle in the wok. Nalini's heart burned with resentment. What woman didn't want to cook for her husband?

'What if Meni's father has married again!' the co-wife would declare from time to time, taking care that her voice reached Nalini's ears. 'He only likes to eat food cooked by me. "You are the mistress, and the household is yours," he says. "I brought the other one to help you in your work."'

Abodh Das didn't own any land. After Partition he went into business with his childhood friend Mofizzul. They were two of a kind. They were good boatmen and their job was rowing people from this side of the river to the other and vice versa. There was a lot of buying and selling going on. Lungis, gamchhas and vests, even cattle loaded on trucks, would be smuggled from India and sold by Abodh. Who were the buyers? Nalini wondered. She realized that it was a risky business.

'Why do you worry?' Her mother-in-law waved her fears away. 'We eat well and dress well. My son is a good provider and surrounds us with comforts. What more can we want?'

Nalini's husband, co-wife and mother-in-law were in one camp. Nalini in another. There was only one room in the house. It was divided into two parts with a bamboo screen. Abodh Das and his first wife slept in the larger space. Nalini, her son, and mother-in-law in the smaller one.

Nalini's mother would come to see her once in a while. 'You have a grandson now,' Abodh's mother would taunt her, 'and you've come empty handed.'

'You bring a girl from a beggarly family like that one,' Abodh would mutter in his mother-in-law's presence, 'and this is what you'll get.'

And what heaps of gold and silver have you given your only son? The words would rise to Nalini's lips but she dared not utter them. *Nothing … nothing at all*, she thought bitterly. When Naran was six months old, the co-wife had cooked a mess of rice and powdered milk, seated him on her lap, and fed him a spoonful. 'His rice ceremony has been properly conducted,' she had announced pompously. Thoughts like these were gradually corroding Nalini's soul.

Nalini's mother-in-law doted on the child. And, gradually, her initial indifference to her changed into appreciation. 'Daughter after daughter!' she would mutter contemptuously. 'The family line would have died out but for this boy. May he have a glorious future!'

'Leave him with me whenever Bara Bou calls you for some work,' she would whisper in Nalini's ear. 'I'll take care of him.' And to her granddaughters she would say, 'Don't carry your brother about all the time. It's not good for a baby boy. His limbs become slack and weak.'

These thoughts and many others drift in and out of Nalini's head. She was born a girl. And all she had heard in her life was that a girl is a fishbone in everyone's throat.

'So many Hindus have left the land,' her mother would say to her father. 'You have two daughters hanging from your neck. How will you find husbands for them?'

'There are still quite a few families like us in the village. Not all have gone away.'

Baba had met Abodh one day while selling coconuts in the market. Abodh hadn't hidden anything. He was twenty-two years older than the girl. And he had another wife and two daughters at home. But it was his sacred duty to help a fellow human being in distress. Besides, he needed a son.

'I earn enough money to keep two wives in comfort,' he assured his future father-in-law, 'and I won't insist on a big dowry. Give her whatever clothes and jewels you can afford.

And there's no need to send her to me immediately after the wedding. Keep her with you till she's old enough to do the household chores.'

No. Abodh Das hadn't left the country. Like many others he had stayed on.

That was all. 'Get up, girl. You're to be wed,' was the next thing she heard.

When sending her to her marital home her father had given her four saris, two petticoats, two tape bodices and four blouses. In the seven years that she had stayed with her husband she had earned one sari each year. The thought made her heart burn. One sari each year for all the back breaking work she had done!

'What about the boy's education?' Abodh's old mother would nag her son. 'You could have gone to Bongaon when so many others did but you refused to leave. What'll you do now?' Abodh listened quietly as a rule. But, at times, he would glare at her with fiery eyes.

Nalini couldn't fathom the reason for the exodus to India that took place in 1965. It came on so suddenly. She had washed a heap of kanthas, mosquito nets, and sheets and hung them out to dry. Then, just as she was taking down a bundle of firewood from the machan, she heard a shrill cry. 'O re O Abodh!' her mother-in-law shrieked. 'Everyone is leaving and you're sitting at home whispering *phusur, phusur* in Bara Bou's ears. What are you two planning? To dump us here and run away? Who will save the boy? And your daughters? Will you allow the Moslahs to drag them away and rape them?

At these words Abodh turned into a beast. He came out of the room, his eyes flaming with hate. 'If it comes to that, I'll kill my wives and daughters. I'll press my foot on their throats till the air gushes out of their lungs.'

It was then that Nalini's mother-in-law had advised her to run away with her son. 'Pack your jewels in a fold of your sari close to your stomach and go. I don't like the way Abodh is behaving. I fear for your safety…'

Nalini's eyes stared into the dark. The year was sixty-five, not seventy-one, the year Pakistan got divided. Yet so many people left. When she arrived at the camp in Ashok Nagar, Howrah, she saw hundreds of refugees like her. She was puzzled. It was her husband who organized the movement of people from this country to the other. Yet she had to walk for miles with her seven-year-old son. Dragging him along or carrying him.

She had stayed in the camp for several months before Gobindo's father had come for them. Abodh hadn't left the village. That was the last thing she heard before she lost touch with him. She was twenty-five then. She was sixty-three today. Nalini's lips curled in a half-smile. Thirty-eight years had gone by but she hadn't crumbled. She was still standing on her feet.

What would she have done if the woman sleeping in her room hadn't stood by her?

'Why don't you have a house of your own, Didi?' Nalini used to ask Mukundo'r Ma.

'First Gobindo's father, then Gobindo, took everything. I didn't come empty handed … let me tell you that. I brought everything I had. Today, I have nothing. My sons work for him, get beaten and sent to jail. He bails them out and puts them to work again. I have sinned, Nalini. That's why I'm being punished.'

'Why do you say that?'

'I believed them. Father and son. I couldn't protect my children. Was that not a sin?'

Thoughts long forgotten, swim around in Nalini's mind. The night ends…

Morning

Dugga! Dugga! Mukundo'r Ma sits up. She hands Bubi some money and says, 'Go to the teashop and buy a pot of tea. Tell your mother to wash and clean the house. People will start coming soon.'

Nalini looks at her with dazed eyes. 'Don't worry. I'll take care of you,' the other woman assures her.

'Is she allowed to drink tea?' Bubi's mother mutters, shooting a glance at her mother-in-law. Her face is long and sullen.

'Why not? It's an old habit of hers. Besides she hasn't seen the man in thirty-eight years. He has never even bothered to find out if his son is alive or dead.'

'I don't know. A widow isn't...'

'Ore O Nalini!' Mukundo'r Ma lets out a hoot of laughter. 'Your daughter-in-law is talking as though Madan Gosain's wife has turned widow. Look here, Bou. It's Nalini who has reared your co-wife's son. Neither you nor your husband have ever given him a thought. You came in such haste not because a father-in-law you've never seen is dead. You're here to grab the old woman's house and sell it to Gobindo. But it won't be that easy. We're with her.'

The daughter-in-law pulls a long face. 'Well,' she mutters, 'the basic rites must be carried out, at least. The widow, her son, and grandson must observe *ashouch* for ten days. Eat *hobishyi* once a day cooked in a *malsha* and...'

'Hobishyi! She works as a maid from dawn to dusk. She barely earns enough to afford two square meals a day. What's more, you've dumped your son on her. And you expect her to ... Leave it. I'll go home now, bathe and do my puja. I won't be long. You must take a bath, Nalini, and wash away your sindoor. But drink your tea first. I'll come with you to the ghat.'

The daughter-in-law shuts her mouth.

'Were you able to sleep, Thakma?' Bubi asks.

'A little. Look, I'll give you some money. Go to the telephone booth and call Dada and Ginni Ma. Tell them I can't come for a few days. Tell them not to worry. I'll get back to work as soon as I can. And bring me your new dhuti and the blouse I washed yesterday. They should serve well enough.'

Mukundo'r Ma returns. 'Gobindo is making elaborate arrangements for the sraddha,' she smirks snidely. 'He has a cunning plan. He'll pay for everything and in return you'll give him your house.'

'For whose corpse is he arranging the sraddha? His father's? Come, Didi, let's go to the ghat.'

Naran was deeply offended by Nalini's manner. He was her only son and she was bypassing him altogether. He and his wife quickly formed a camp of their own. Who would have guessed that they'd had a terrible fight only last night?

'I'll cut you into pieces,' the husband had shouted.

'I went to the police the other day,' the wife shouted back, 'and filed a report. If you touch me with so much as your little finger, they'll haul you off to jail.'

Today they were looking at each other with bewildered eyes. They suffered from a mutual affliction.

At this point Bubi walked into the room and opened the trunk in which his grandmother kept her belongings. 'Take a new thala from the trunk and give it to your Thakma,' his father instructed the boy. Bubi didn't reply. Taking his dhuti and his grandmother's blouse and petticoat he walked out of the room.

'What sort of son is he? Doesn't obey his father!'

'Beimaan er bachcha!' The loving father gnashed his teeth.

'You called yourself a beimaan?'

'Stop it, woman. Prattle, prattle, prattle. Chewing my head off all the time! Don't you understand that if the sraddha isn't properly conducted the curse will fall on us? We won't find husbands for our daughters.'

'I understand well enough. It's your turn to understand.'

'She hasn't shed a single tear. He was her husband after all...'

'Poor man! I feel sorry for him. To have been married to a scrawny old woman like that one!'

*

Nalini steps into the pond, pushes aside the hyacinth leaves, and takes a dip. She pulls off her plastic bangles and iron hoop and drops them in the water. Scrubbing the sindoor with her forefinger she washes it away. In whose name had she applied sindoor on her parting for thirty-eight years? And why? She wonders...

The pond belonged to the Naskars once. Now it was Gobindo's. Not only the pond. A number of fields around it.

'He is acquiring all the land in the village,' Nalini mutters. 'He'll ask for my house next.'

'He'll try his best. But you mustn't nod your head meekly and say, "Yes Baba."'

'Is it true that women of our caste must follow so many rules and regulations when they're widowed?'

'Nonsense. Rules and regulations indeed! As if the dead man was a king or an emperor! Look, I've been here for many years. I know what is to be done. I'll take you to Kalighat and get all the necessary rituals conducted.'

'What's the expense...?'

'People pay whatever they can. I'll get you a good bargain. Come out of the water now. Gobindo will be arriving soon. He'll try to bully you but you must remain firm.'

'If I can't keep my house...'

'Don't worry. You'll keep it'

The two women returned to see that the rooms had been cleaned and Bubi had spread a mat on the floor. Even as they entered, they heard Naran ordering his son in a hectoring voice. 'Ask your Thakma for some money. A lot of people will be coming. We'll have to give them tea and...'

'Go buy the tea yourself,' Mukundo'r Ma snapped. '*A ha ha ha!* You think your mother is sitting on a mountain of gold. Have you forgotten the day you stole all her savings and disappeared? You haven't shown your face to her for the last fifteen years. When your son was ill it was her neighbours who took him to the hospital. Now that you think you've got a chance to rob the poor woman again, you've come running back.'

'How many kicks will you put up with?' Nalini's daughter-in-law said to her husband. 'That, too, from outsiders? Forget it. Leave them to do what they like.'

'One more word,' Naran glared at her, 'and I'll press my foot on your throat and squeeze your life out.'

'That's the kind of language your father was good at.' Nalini spoke for the first time. 'Worthy son of a worthy father! I can't deny that it's your duty to perform your father's last rites. But if you've come with the intention of stealing the roof above my head...'

She couldn't complete her sentence. Gobindo walked in.

'I've brought Suraj.' He shot a glance at Nalini. 'He conducts the rituals for your caste. He'll tell you what to do.

You don't have faith in me. Very good. Naran, come and sit with us. Listen carefully to what he has to say. Begin, Suraj…'

'Let me see,' Suraj, the temple priest, began ponderously. 'The death occurred about twenty days ago…'

'Twenty-three,' Gobindo corrected him. 'If one includes today … it's twenty-four.'

Suraj fixed a stern eye on Nalini. 'You've eaten fish all these days … I suppose,' he said.

'Of course,' Mukundo'r Ma's voice cut in like a blade of ice. 'She eats seven-course meals every day with chunks of fish! If she has eaten any, it might be a few shrimps or minnows.'

'What or how much she has eaten is of no consequence. She has sinned and must atone for it. If not, retribution will surely follow. Besides…'

'Why?' Mukundo'r Ma interrupted. 'Did she know her husband was dead when she put a pinch of fish in her mouth? There's no sin in it.'

'Look, Mashi. If you keep interrupting like this…'

Nalini had been silent all this while. Now she spoke up. 'Let me handle this, Didi,' she said, her voice gentle but firm. 'Look, Suraj,' she continued, 'I won't beat about the bush. I'm asking you straight off. How much do you expect me to spend?'

'Well…' Suraj screwed up his eyes in serious calculation. 'There's the atonement part of it. Then the sraddha. That alone will come to seven or eight hundred rupees. At my lowest quote…'

'What else?'

'The men of the clan have to be fed. If you can give them a proper meal, well and good. If not, chirey, curd, fruits and sweets will do.'

'I understand. So, tell me, Gobindo … how much in all?'

'Well. There's the widow's white to be bought. And all the provisions for thirteen days hobishyanno. There are so many members in your family...'

'How much?'

'Well ... about four to five thousand.'

Nalini's mouth curls in a smile. 'And how must I repay this four to five thousand?'

'Look. I'm your well-wisher. A member of your family so to speak. Naran's suggestion is that you mortgage the house...'

'Why doesn't he mortgage his own house and perform his father's sraddha? Who is Naran? What right does he have to decide what I must do? Listen, all of you. I've made a will leaving the house to my grandson. The document is kept in Dada's safe.'

'What about my father's last rites?' Naran roars like a bull.

'I might just offer some til and tulsi here. Or I might go to Kalighat. Whatever is convenient. Let me see...'

'And what about me? You want me to go to hell?'

'It's up to you. You may stay here and eat hobishyi with me for three days. Then go to Kalighat and perform your father's sraddha. And if you feel that's not good enough, go home and organize a daan sagar for your revered father.'

'What about you?'

'I'll have to see. I have to think of money.'

The faces surrounding the new widow turn to stone. The silence lasts a long while. Till Gobindo cries out in an anguished voice, 'Hai! Hai! I have spent so much money already! I've bought black-bordered dhutis, rice and raw bananas for your hobishyanno. What you're doing is wrong, Mashi. You'll go to hell...'

'If it comes to that ... I don't mind. I had a husband who abandoned me for forty years. A son who sees my condition with his own eyes yet wants to snatch the roof over my head. I live in hell even now. How much worse can the other hell be? Go to the market, Naran. Buy rice, raw bananas, malshas and whatever other stuff is needed. Take the money from me. As for you Gobindo ... go home. I've been alone all these years and will remain alone for the rest of my life. I'll conduct my husband's sraddha the way I wish.'

The crowd disperses. There are threats and abuses in loud voices. But Nalini is unmoved.

'Didi,' she turns to Mukundo'r Ma, 'I'll go to my employers tomorrow and ask for an advance. They'll give it. We'll go to Kalighat after three days and perform the sraddha. Then, if there's some money left, we'll feed four or five poor families. If I can't afford a proper meal, I'll give them chirey, batasha and curd.'

'O re O Nalini! I never thought you could muster the courage to go against your own...'

'Who's my own, Didi? Whose sraddha must I spend my hard-earned money on? And why? Who'll feed me if I lose my job? I'll have to starve or beg in the streets.'

It is thus that Nalini sets a new standard for herself. Brings a new meaning to her life.

Shonkhomala

Manohar Mouli Biswas

All his life Manush Dom had fought against overwhelming odds. Battered by one assault after another in the struggle for existence, he was left crushed and defeated. Why his parents had named him Manush (Man) he did not know. For, though human, he had had to endure dishonour and humiliation every day. He had been treated like an animal.

A daughter of surpassing beauty had been born to him. And out of a great flow of filial love, Manush had named her Shonkhomala … a garland of conch shells. It was an unsuitable name for the daughter of a dom but truly her skin was as white and gleaming as a conch and her voluptuous form as graceful as a swaying garland. How this gleaming beauty metamorphosed into an evil spirit lurking in the dark shadows of a bamboo clump, is what this story is all about.

Manush Dom lived in an obscure village not very far from Singur. His parents were very poor. All they had was an acre and a half of arable land which they farmed for a living. Theirs was a large family and they eked out a precarious existence. Despite the many privations they had to undergo, they were honest and upright people. No one had ever accused any of them of cheating or theft.

A number of genteel families lived in Singur. They were educated folk and held high posts with the government. Many of them had sent their children abroad to study in the universities of Great Britain, Europe, America and Canada. These people, from the upper strata of the Hindu caste system, were convinced that doms were thieves. If not, they argued, why would a great writer like Tarashankar write his excellent story *Chor-er Ma* (The Thief's Mother) about Shashi Dom?

An idea, once it takes root, is very difficult to dislodge. *Doms are thieves.* The conviction is embedded in the minds of many upper-caste people. If Manush Dom went from door to door, with snakes twined around his neck, touched his head to the ground and pleaded with his neighbours, 'We are not thieves. Please believe us,' he wouldn't succeed in changing their minds.

A writer of Tarashankar's eminence wouldn't write such a story if he wasn't sure of his facts ... would he?

Who would dare pass over Tarashankar's view in favour of Manush Dom's?

As Shonkhomala grew to be a woman, her fair skin, cloud of dark hair, luminous eyes and the swan-like grace with which her bare feet glided over the paddy fields, caught the eyes of many. Hearts heaved and beat fast at the sight of her. Yet a slight doubt, an uncertainty marred the perception of beauty that rose in every male breast. She was gorgeous of course, no one could deny that, and her voluptuous body was meant to be enjoyed. But only in secrecy. Away from the eyes of others. She was a dom's daughter, after all, and marrying her was out of the question. Even more so was the notion of bringing her home as a bride. An act like that would be repugnant in the eyes of the village folk. They wouldn't sit still and allow it. No. Never.

It was true, of course, that village elders advocated marriage; even exhorted young men to marry and perpetuate their lineage. But only with the strictest adherence to caste and creed. These were pre-eminent requisites in marriage. Grace, beauty, intelligence and talent came last. Custom and tradition had to be preserved at all costs and it was only through marriage that this was possible. Allowing a way of life, that had existed through centuries, to crumble and die was unthinkable.

Vedic dharma propagates the preservation of caste and colour. It is like an oyster imprisoned in its own shell...

Who will dare to make a dent in the iron-bound structure set up by the Vedas three thousand years ago? The tradition of caste apartheid flourishes, to this day, in full and pompous glory. Marriage outside one's caste is deemed to be worse than death. Shonkhomala's lovely face and billowing youth have attracted many. But apart from professing undying love they have done little else. No one has had the courage to offer marriage.

Shonkhomala knows that her beauty and accomplishments will not help her find a space other than the one ordained for her three thousand years ago. Though she hasn't received much education, she has only cleared her School Final Exams, she has a fund of natural intelligence quite rare in her community. She understands and accepts the reality of her position.

When the time came to wed her, Manush Dom scoured his own village and others around it in search of a suitable groom. The periphery of his search wasn't vastly extensive. It lay within a few villages in Hooghly district. Singur and its environs. After a long search his choice fell on a young man named Harikanta Dom.

The surname Dom is obnoxious. To hear it is to feel aversion and contempt. Upper-caste folk abhor the caste so much, they are afraid to step into a dom's shadow. If a member of the slighted community goes to one of their houses, he is made to stand in the yard and explain his presence from a safe distance.

But things have started to change. Doms have begun questioning the wisdom of proclaiming their caste through their names. *Why should we wear the badge of shame, thrust upon us by a cruel social order, on our sleeves?* they ask themselves. They are thinking of ways and means to shake off the stigma.

Harikanta was illiterate. He had never set foot across the threshold of a school. Though moderately intelligent he was somewhat timorous and cowardly. Too trusting. People could take him for a ride quite easily. At the party office which he visited from time to time … it was difficult to survive in the village if one didn't do *some* work for the party … he believed every word that was said to him. 'Your name is on record in the official documents,' the party babus told him. 'You belong to the Scheduled Caste. Why do you or any of your caste need an education?'

Harikanta and Shonkhomala were wed on an auspicious night and the two made a happy home together. The illiterate husband had the deepest respect for his young wife's learning. Marvelling at the ease with which she read books and newspapers, he listened carefully to everything she said and paid heed to all her advice.

One day, Shonkhomala said to him, 'Do you know that, somewhere on this earth, there is a place called Sindh?' When he shook his head, she continued. 'There's a district in it called Larkana. Larkana is supposed to be the repository of an ancient civilization … perhaps the oldest in the world. There's another stretch of land close to it called Punjab. It has a district which, during British rule, was called Montgomery. Montgomery has an equally ancient civilization. We, who are called doms today, and considered the lowest of the low, derive our roots from it. And those who hate and despise us actually come from a later, much lesser civilization. It is called the Aryan civilization. The Vedas are Aryan texts. Why should we, who come from an older, superior line bow our heads before people who came after us? Who lived in jungles when we were living in towns and cities?'

Harikanta listened to his young wife in amazed silence. As if wrapped in the soft dark layers of a faraway world. A dream world. Suddenly his head shot up. 'You're right, Shonkhomala. You're right!' he cried out in what was almost like a shout. 'You know why?' He sat up in his excitement. 'Because I've just realized that I'm no different from the men, the high-caste babus, I serve. At the flag-hoisting ceremony on Independence Day or at any other ceremony, don't I raise my voice in the national anthem same as they do? Don't our voices mingle together in the words *Punjab, Sindh, Gujarat, Maratha, Dravid, Utkal, Banga*? Why are Punjab and Sindh named first in the list? Because theirs is the older civilization. They came before the rest. Even before Banga.'

Harikanta had received no education at all but his wife had. Not much of course. But enough to set her apart from other girls of the dom community. Passing the School Final examination was a big thing. Under her gentle guidance, Harikanta learned a great deal about the history of the country in which they lived, its many cultures and traditions. He also picked up the art of expressing his thoughts.

'We didn't come flying from another planet,' he said, one day, with a new urgency in his voice. 'We are heirs to a civilization far older than the one we bow our heads to. We are this land's original inhabitants. We were here far before the ones who lord it over us, even heard of it. We were their maliks. Masters. Come, let us cast off the surname that brings us only shame and dishonour. My name, from today, is not Harikanta Dom. It is Harikanta Malik. And yours is Shonkhomala Malik.'

'That is a good idea,' Shonkhomala answered solemnly. 'But the other side will not accept it. They will never forget that we are doms.'

Harikanta: We will change our surnames ... nevertheless.

Shonkhomala: Yes. And our first names too. We will forge new identities for ourselves.

Harikanta: You're absolutely right. I find your name too long and difficult to pronounce. I can't get my tongue around it properly.

Shonkhomala: What name do you propose for yourself?

Harikanta: I'm an ordinary man. Simple and uncomplicated. I don't understand many things. The babus in the party office often tell me that I'm an ignoramus. They call me Bholanath. It is Shiva's name. A good name. I've decided I'll be called Bholanath Malik from this day onwards.

Shonkhomala: Like the wife of Shiva I, too, went through a period of austerity, prayer and penance to win my Bholanath. Let my name be Tapashi.

Harikanta's head shot up. Raising his voice, he cried out, 'My name is Bholanath Malik and my wife's name is Tapashi Malik.'

His voice was so loud and imperious, so unlike Harikanta's timid diffident one, that the neighbours came running to see what ailed him.

*

Harikanta wasn't a poor man. He was the owner of three-and-a-half acres of land and one acre of forest in which bamboo and cane grew in profusion. The land, which he farmed with his own hands, was fertile and yielded a good crop of paddy twice a year.

He had four children. Two sons and two daughters. The village school was not a good one. The teachers were lax and negligent and took classes when they felt like it. No examinations were conducted. What little the children had learned had been through their own efforts and that of their mother.

The family followed their caste profession. Shonkhomala and her daughters cut cane from the woods and trimmed and dried them in the sun. They stripped the peels off bamboo lengths and wove them into a variety of baskets, trays for winnowing rice, and even shaped them into pitchers and vases. Mother and daughters worked hard all day and father and sons took their produce, every Wednesday morning, to sell at the weekly haat. There was no lack of food or, indeed, any other kind of deprivation in Shonkhomala's household. They were a happy, contented family.

One day, Harikanta returned from the party office with a worried expression on his face. The babus had informed him that the Tatas were building a motor car factory and were taking possession of land in and around Singur. Since Harikanta's three-and-a-half acres fell within the area they were in the process of acquiring, he had to sign a form giving permission. Illiterate as he was, he had signed the form without knowing what he was doing.

But the moment Shonkhomala and his children heard of this they cried out in shock, 'No. Never. We won't give up our land. Why should we? It is our land. It sustains us all year round. What use will a motor car factory be to us?'

'The party babus said that once the factory is built, Singur will become a flourishing town,' Harikanta muttered feebly. 'A lot of rich people will build houses here. They will need servants and will pay well. Our village women can make good money working for them. As for the men, they will find employment in the factory. Or if they wish, they can set up shops selling tea, paan or groceries with the compensation they will receive. With the growth of the town, they will do a roaring business.'

Harikanta was a simple man. He simply parroted what the babus has said to him without giving it a second thought.

But Shonkhomala Dom, alias Shonkhomala Malik, alias Tapashi Malik was made of sterner stuff. Dismissing her husband's explanations with an impatient wave of her hand, she stood up. 'Get all our neighbours together,' she commanded her children. 'Go from door to door and tell everyone to assemble in our bamboo grove this evening. We must have a meeting.'

A lot of people could be seen in Harikanta's bamboo grove that evening. All those who were against giving up their land were there. 'Brothers and sisters,' Shonkhomala opened the meeting, 'the party babus will try to make you change your minds. They will tempt you with many promises. But please understand that a motor car factory, in place of the good arable land our ancestors have farmed for generations, will be of no use to us. Our boys have little education. What work will they do in the factory? The babus are aiding and abetting the Tatas to benefit their own sons. Many of them hold engineering degrees but have remained unemployed for years. The factory will come in useful for them. Why should we give up our land for *their* welfare?'

There was a murmur of agreement. Shonkhomala now pointed to a man who stood quietly at the edge of the throng.

'This gentleman,' she said, 'is a poet and a true friend of the poor. Many of you have heard of Bhavatosh Satpathy of Medinipur and his famous lines…' She commenced reciting them in a strong resonant voice ringing with authority:

I am the poet of the oppressed
Not of the times
Tearing my Brahminic thread with a cry of pain
I've become a Chandal
I've renounced the Vedas and flung in the Sindhu,
all caste differences thereof
Shaving my head in reverence
I am merged with the poor of the land.

'We are Chandals. We have the strength of our caste. We will give our heart's blood … but not our land. Our land is our mother. It feeds us. Our land is our father. It protects us. Let us all stand together and take a pledge. Let us say in one voice, *we will give our flesh and blood but not the land that has nurtured and cherished us for generations. We will not abandon the source and sustenance of our lives.*'

There was a roar of applause from the people present. The whole of Singur resonated with the cry. *We will not give up our land. No. Never.*

It was decided that a great procession, opposing the move, would be taken out the next day.

At early dawn a band of goons barged into Harikanta's house and carried off Shonkhomala. She was gang-raped in her own bamboo grove and murdered. Pouring petrol over her dead body they burned it to ashes.

No one was arrested for this grisly crime. The police didn't have a clue as to who committed it or who was behind it.

The compensation money reached many hands, bit by bit, before it came to Harikanta ... a fraction of what had been promised.

Harikanta and his children have left the village. No one knows where they are. No one has bothered to make enquiries, either. As for Shonkhomala, she has turned into an evil spirit whom everyone fears. No one dares walk through the bamboo grove which she guards with all the power of her metamorphosed state.

Snake Maiden

Prafulla Kumar Roy

Sonai Bibi-r Bil. A low-lying fen in a remote corner of the earth far away from the hustle and bustle of everyday life. In the bitter cold of winter, when winds from the north blow hard and dry, Sonai Bibi-r Bil shrivels into herself like the rotting carcass of an old woman. All that is visible are her skeletal remains. Patches of water, green with scum, shimmer between masses of earth risen from her breast. And around them, as far as the eye can see, are unending sweeps of wild reeds, bulrushes and tussock grass. There are deep shadows here. Shadows and silence. Water and verdure are locked together in restful sleep.

When the first monsoon showers fall upon the earth Sonai Bibi-r Bil awakes. Shaking off her torpor, she raises her face to the sky and drinks great gulps of pelting rain. Her contours change. She stretches and expands. Her newly awakened limbs unfurl and spread in all directions. To the north, south, east and west ... all the way to the horizon. The Meghna helps her. Swelling and frothing in a demonic dance she bursts her banks and makes her way into the fen. Wrapping her in a fierce embrace she turns her into a great sheet of waving water. Sensuous, joyous, seductive…

Then, after autumn has waned and the fierce frosty winds of hemanta have raped and battered her voluptuous form, Sonai Bibi-r Bil turns into a sad, withered replica of her once glorious self. The sap of youth drains away from her limbs and, who knows from what dark depths, stretches of virgin soil appear.

Winter follows. And now flocks of birds … katora, imli, jalpipi and innumerable others … come flying in from distant shores. They have many names. Many colours. Descending on her in sweeps, they turn Sonai Bibi-r Bil into a rainbow. With them come other migratory creatures. Bedeys, nomadic snake charmers, anchor their boats in her shallow waters. The sound of rushing wings and soft footfalls enters her ears. Delicious tremors rise from deep within, and her land and water sway and shiver with ecstasy.

That they are here this winter, too, is evident from the many tents that have blossomed like land lotuses all over Sonai Bibi-r Bil. Other flowers can be seen. Along with the krishnakali that dapples the breast of the fen with clutches of purple stars are the snake maidens. These are winsome creatures in motley-coloured skirts rippling seductively from narrow waists to slim ankles. Bunches of golden flowers wave coyly from tangled locks. Their eyes are long and languorous. But, at times, a sudden flame can spurt into a dark iris and flicker and dance like the head of a deadly cobra. They wear ornaments made from the bones of snakes and birds. Imli-wing necklaces and kuchila-spine bracelets adorn long necks and arms. Danglers, fashioned from the delicate neck bones of a shankha naag, swing from tiny earlobes.

The short days of winter provide a welcome rest for the nomads, a brief diversion in their wandering lives. A time to suspend floating over turbulent waters and experience the joy of putting down roots. To revel in the comfort and security enjoyed by the householder. Naagmati bedeyni's snake maidens sit all day long, basking in warm sunshine, weaving trays and baskets. The men squatting beside them peel reeds and twine tufts of tussock grass into ropes. They are young men with stone-hard limbs and staring eyes … crimson from mahua wine. Their rough tawny manes are tied with lengths of entrails pulled out of chakrachoor snakes and dried to ribbons. Dark lips are parted in foolish smiles. But not all are employed thus. Some pursue more arduous tasks. Stealing sheaves of mustard, sesame and kaon paddy from the waving fields on three sides of the fen, is one of them. Stalking wild geese and bringing them down with skilled throws of sharp-edged harpoons is another.

They come every winter. Winter stretches into spring on the wings of mellow breezes. Summer follows. The parched earth bakes and cracks, raising swirls of scorching dust. Still, the call to resume their roving lives doesn't reach their ears. But when the first monsoon clouds rise from the horizon and cool winds laden with moisture come wafting into Sonai Bibi-r Bil, they shake off their languor and ready themselves for their tryst with the waiting waters. Sails are unfurled and oars mended. Towing ropes stretch and tighten in muscled palms. Muttering fervent prayers to Allah and Bishohari, their preferred name for the snake goddess Manasa, they set sail once more. Frail barks ride high on the waves as the ferocious Meghna comes swaying and swerving into Sonai Bibi-r Bil.

Reeds, bulrush, tussock and broom disappear. Sonai Bibi-r Bil turns into a sea of black water. Boats fly over foam-tipped waves and down again. From the Meghna to the Padma. From the Padma to the Kalabadar mooring, from time to time, on alien banks. Then sky and water resonate with the echoes of sharp, sweet voices. *Bish pathor, Ma! Khanti bish pathor! Bishohari-r doai shob bish uithya aashbo. Dudhraj, Chandrachud, Aalad, Gokkhur ... Jodhi booti niba, Ma? Jodhi booti?* (Poison stones, Mistress! Genuine poison stones! Blessed by Bishohari herself. Guaranteed to draw out every trace of poison ... be it that of adder, krait, python or cobra. Herbs and roots, Mistress? Herbs and roots?)

Snake maidens hawking their wares. Calling out to the village women. To wives and mothers...

Hopes and dreams rise in heaving breasts. The nesting instinct pulls at their heartstrings. A slumberous numbness creeps into their veins and blood flows slow and heavy as though scented with opium flowers. The mind begins to send out roots and tendrils. But as soon as the sky darkens with cloud and rain comes pelting down, they remember their ancestral promise to the waters of the earth and resume their drifting, roving lives.

*

This winter morning, as on all others, they sit with their backs turned to the sweet warm sun, weaving dried grass and reeds into bins and baskets to be sold by the men at the weekly market in Kamalaganj. Their hands work swiftly for soon it will be time for them to walk down the village paths with their pouches of poison stones and baskets of snakes. To persuade wives and mothers to buy their herbs and roots, potions, charms and amulets. To entertain the villagers by making the deadliest snakes dance to their pipes. To return with fistfuls of silver joy...

Sonai Bibi-r Bil resonates with quick voices and shrill laughter. Mohabbat looks up from his task of peeling a bamboo cane and turns to one of the younger girls. '*Ki lo, Palanki*?' he asks with a mocking smile. 'Where is Shankhini this morning? She's not to be seen anywhere. Has her position of Amma turned her into a star in the sky?'

Shankhini is, presently, the mistress of this band of bedeys. The Queen Bee. Comments like these are tantamount to treason. Besides, no one has the right to take her name. She must be addressed as Amma. She can, if she wishes, split any heart in two with a deadly thrust of her javelin. But Mohabbat is foolish and reckless. Quite often he forgets his place.

Palanka darts a timid glance at Mohabbat. There is something about her that sets her apart from the other girls. She is like a wild flower, small and humble, that knows it was born in the dust. Her eyes are misty with a faraway look in them. A scent, faint and sweet as a musk deer's, rises from her limbs. It spreads around and beyond her like a cloud, soothing and calming all those who come near her. Eyes grow soft when they meet hers and the soul is filled with tranquility.

She has no answer to Mohabbat's question. Her heart beats fast and she lowers her eyes. Another woman is quick to respond. A cackle of fierce laughter bursts from Aatarjaan's lips ... so loud and bitter that the heart of the fen trembles with fear. Aatarjaan's body is tight and well formed, but her face is black and crumpled as though ravaged by a phantom fire. '*O re*, Mohabattya! Spawn of a slave!' she shrieks, her ugly mouth twisted in contempt. 'The nesting fever has gripped our Shankhini. Don't you know? She is wearing a red sari and has smeared sindoor on her brow and parting. She is standing before a mirror admiring herself. Go take a look. *Hee Hee Hee*!' Turning to the girl she screeches with laughter, '*Ki lo, Palanki*. You're pining for a home and husband too ... aren't you? Go ... go. Turn yourself into a wife and mother, you slut. *Hee Hee Hee*!'

Five boats containing all the necessities of a nomadic life stand anchored in the shallow waters. An angry growl is heard from one of them. '*Ke? Ke?*' Shankhini's booming voice hits the ears like a clap of thunder. '*Ei* Mohabbatya, you dirty jinn! *Ei* Aatar ... you whore! I'm coming ... Just wait and see what I do. I'll slaughter you two instead of a hen and drink your blood.'

Shankhini storms in, her young body swift as a flash of lightning. The sindoor in the parting of her hair blazes like a streaking flame. Deep red silk flows around her limbs like a river of blood. Her magnificent breasts, heaving with passion, move up and down with every fierce breath. Her long eyes glitter like the spitting tongue of a deadly krait.

The fire goes out of Mohabbat. Aatarjaan trembles and turns pale. The rest of the band are struck dumb with terror. Only Palanka gazes at Shankhini with wistful eyes. An intense yearning rises from deep within her at the sight of Naagmati bedeyni's fiery daughter in a sari and sindoor. The humble flower's eyes fill with tears. Her heart is consumed with longing.

A scent, fresh and earthy, comes wafting into her soul as though from a vast distance. It brings promise of love and protection. Of peace and stability. Somewhere, in some alien village, someone is waiting for her. A man with a broad chest on which she rests her head in sweet surrender. A child is suckling at her breast. She feels his soft damp mouth tugging at her nipple, sending tremors of joy running through her frame. She sees a tiny hut with a vine growing over the thatch. Bunches of beans, speckled with gold dust, dance in the breeze. A yard, neatly swabbed with cow dung is surrounded by mango and lemon trees. Doves fly in and out of their shadows and sing from their branches on warm somnolent afternoons.

Walking through the villages bordering the Meghna, Padma and Ilsha, Palanka has seen these scenes. She has heard the legend, integral to their worship of Manasa, of how Behula had sailed over these waters with her dead husband Lakhai till she reached the abode of the gods and persuaded them to bring him back to life. This great stretch of land and water is rendered holy, to this day, by Behula's chastity.

Palanka's dream of a peaceful nest in some obscure corner of the earth, of lifelong faith and trust in a man she calls *husband*, has made her drifting blood yearn to drop anchor. *Perhaps the same dream has begun to haunt Shankhini*, she muses wistfully. *To beckon to her with shadowy fingers*. Even so, Palanka knows there is no escape for her. She is a slave to Shankhini's will. Dozens of eyes guard her all the time.

Shankhini glares at the assembled men and women. Her brows are knitted together like a pair of scorpions. Her slender limbs, swathed in crimson, rages like a forest fire. Tongues of flame dart from her eyes. She looks like a wild falcon ready to swoop on her detractors and tear their flesh to shreds with her talons. But before she can do anything, a whirlwind comes spinning through the bushes.

'Amma! Amma!' A fearful voice pierces her ears as Sikandar comes charging in, his flying feet trampling reeds and grass. 'Disaster has befallen us,' he cries. 'Another band is in the fen. They have anchored their boats on the opposite side. I saw them myself...'

The irises of Shankhini's eyes change colour. They take on the tawny hue of a tigress lurking behind a keya clump whose spiky leaves and towers of flowers exude a pungent sweetness.

'Zulfikar!' she hollers, her voice echoing like a roll of thunder.

Zulfikar, chief of Shankhini's warrior band, is lounging some distance away in the shade of some screw pine bushes. He has been drinking a local brew since morning and, by now, his stomach has swelled up like a barrel. He hears his mistress call out his name. There is something so immediate, so urgent, in her voice that his dim drowsy senses are shocked into a sudden awakening. The bottle gets knocked out of his hand and its contents spill out in spurts on the grass.

He rises to his feet. He is a huge hulk of a man. His face, which seems cut out of a giant slab of coal, is devoid of brows and lashes, and his jawbones jut out like mountain crags. Hibiscus-red eyes glare malignantly. *Grrrrrr* ... a roar, like that of a lion rudely aroused from sleep, gathers in his throat and bursts from his mouth. It is a war cry. The peace and serenity of the winter morning is shattered. Hands stop their work and senses tense at the sound.

In this land of swamp and river there was an unwritten law. No one knew who had thought of it first, or when, but it was part of a code of conduct followed by all bedeys irrespective of where they came from. *No band ventured into a space already occupied by another.*

Zulfikar had arrived on the scene by now. Mohabbat, Sikandar and the other men stood up. The women had risen too. The air was filled with hissing sounds as the angry breath left their nostrils. Snake maidens had turned into snakes...

The golden glory of the winter morning dimmed as though dark clouds had swooped on it with clashing wings. Everyone rushed to the boat where the band's weapons were stored. Shankhini forgot her threat of tearing Mohabbat and Aatarjaan, limb from limb, and drinking their blood. Only Palanka sat immobile beside a heap of broom and dried grass. Conflict of any kind terrified her. Her heart quivered like that of a new-born egret. She shut her eyes in fear.

A sudden commotion startled Palanka. She opened her eyes to see Zulfikar marching towards the other side of the fen, a mighty lance held aloft in his hand. Shankhini was behind him followed by Aatarjaan, Dohor Bibi, Moina and the others. From Sikandar and Mohabbat to the youngest boatman … she could see the entire band. A contingent of men and women armed with weapons. Spears, axes and javelins glittered in the sun. Lengths of bamboo swung from powerful hands. The smell of death was in the air. Palanka held her breath till Zulfikar and his army disappeared behind a screen of trees.

The other group of bedeys had arrived only a couple of days ago. They hadn't found time yet to put up their tents and settle down. As they stood surrounded by piles of bamboo and canvas, baskets of snakes and bundles of cooking vessels, a menacing roar reached their ears. *Ei bandi-r poot. Abba Amma-r shaadi dekhtey aichhos? Kalija phainrha dimu.* (Sons of slaves! Have you come here to celebrate the nuptials of your parents? I'll tear your hearts into shreds.)

They looked up startled. A man of colossal dimensions stood before them. His mighty head nearly touched the sky. He was whirling a lance whose glittering edge seemed to be slavering at the mouth for blood. Some of the men ran towards the boats anchored haphazardly in the shallow waters. Others stared at the black mountain with bewildered eyes.

Now another voice rang in the air. 'Sons of whores!' Shankhini let out a yell that matched Zulfikar's in power. 'This is our fen. We come here every year. If you don't disappear this minute, we'll slit your bellies and pull the guts out.'

A deafening silence followed. But it didn't last long. Shankhini's adversaries had armed themselves in a twinkling and now they marched towards her with fire in their eyes and spikes and iron bars in their hands. The two armies advanced. Both were ready for battle.

A deadly combat could have followed. Heads, sliced from bodies, could have rolled on the forest floor. The waters of the fen could have turned crimson with blood. Hearts, lungs and livers could have been cut to pieces.

But the clash was averted by a voice from one of the boats, deep as thunder but astonishingly musical. Both groups froze in their tracks as a man came walking towards them, arms raised in command. He was six-and-a-half-feet tall with limbs that shone like burnished gold. Raven-black hair fell to his shoulders in sleek shining waves and the vast expanse of his chest looked as though carved out of granite. A rare courage and strength radiated from every pore of his body. Yet his eyes had a faraway look in them. A look that was not of this world.

'Why take up arms?' the deep voice boomed. 'Can't we settle the matter amicably?'

Before anyone could respond, what seemed like a flaming meteor whizzed past Zulfikar and stopped before the dazzling presence. It was Shankhini. Ten years had passed. Ten summers and winters had gone by but she had no difficulty in recognizing him.

'Raja saheb?' she murmured. There was a catch in her voice.

'Who are you?' A pair of arched eyebrows came together.

'I'm Shankhini. Don't you recognize me?'

'You're Shankhini! Is this your band?'

'Yes.' Shankhini's eyes passed slowly over the stranger's frame ... as though seeking something.

'Isn't it extraordinary?' a radiant smile lit up his countenance, 'that we stand here today as enemies with sticks and lances in our hands?' Then, addressing both groups, he said in a commanding voice, 'Drop your weapons. There's no need to fight...'

Shankhini stood staring at him. Her mind had left the present and reverted to the past. When she and the man before her were in the first flush of youth. When he could leap into the swirling waters of the Meghna, split a crocodile's heart in two with his lance, and swim to the bank carrying the creature on his back. When he didn't fear to venture into the densest forests to hunt the spotted leopard and bring the carcass back slung from a pole. When the hint of a conflict made his blood simmer with pleasurable anticipation, and a roar, like a storm cloud's, gathered in his throat. When every muscle of his beautiful body swayed and rippled like the hood of a deadly cobra. Those days were history now. Like fairytales heard long ago. Today, he cringed from a simple fight between two bands. Naagmati bedeyni's daughter gazed at him with wonder in her eyes.

How he has changed … she thought … *What divine snake charmer's flute has subdued the snakes writhing and hissing in his blood?*

They had both been members of Asmani bedeyni's band … so long ago … it seemed as though aeons had passed. A time when Raja saheb's hard, gold, tiger-eyes had softened, as though misted with a film of wine, whenever they met her long dark ones. And Shankhini's heart had hummed, like a young bee's, hovering over a flower, whenever he came into her presence…

And then … disaster struck. A terrible storm in Daulatpur, where they were spending the winter, shattered their fleet of boats. Torn to pieces, they sank to the floor of the raging Padma. Swept away by the current, the members of the band got separated and were carried to who knows what unknown destinations…

Shankhini had tried to forget this painful period of her life and succeeded. But she couldn't forget Raja saheb.

'Look, Shankhini,' Raja saheb said peaceably. 'You were here first. The right is on your side. We'll go away. First thing tomorrow we'll set sail towards Char Sohagi and pitch our tents there. Happy?'

'No. Never!' A sharp exclamation, more like a cry of pain, escaped from Shankhini's throat. 'Don't think of leaving. I'm seeing you after so long. S-o-o long. Can I let you go?'

'But two rival bands can't stay in the same place. I don't like squabbling and fighting. Those days are over…'

'I'm the leader of my band.' Shankhini's eyes blazed with triumph. 'What I say counts. No one from my side will challenge your presence in Sonai Bibi-r Bil.'

Raja saheb shook his head and remained silent.

'Let me ask you a question. What has changed you so? Since when has the thought of conflict become so fearful? Only a few years have gone by since we—'

'I'm weary, Shankhini.' A melancholy smile appeared on Raja saheb's lips. 'I'm weary of this roving life. Here today, there tomorrow. Endlessly warring and killing one another! And for what? A little space in which, according to a rule laid down by our nomadic forefathers, we are forbidden to put down roots. Ordinary folk hate us. Snake charming and selling poison stones don't provide a living any longer. If we steal, we end up in prison. Of what use is this existence? Far better to farm a bit of land somewhere, build a hut and live in peace.'

Shankhini was startled. So were all the others. What was he saying? How could he even dream of disregarding the edict, laid down by Bishohari herself and followed by the nomadic race from time immemorial? What terrible blasphemy! Even hearing such talk was sin! The snake goddess would be outraged!

'Don't utter such words.' Shankhini shuddered. 'Don't utter them ever again! Beware of Bishohari's wrath. She'll send her deadly, conch-skinned snakes to destroy you. *Jai Ma Bishohari!*'

Jai Ma Bishohari! Loud voices echoed hers till sky, water and land resonated with the sound.

Raja saheb's wan smile faded. 'I understand your feelings, Shankhini,' he said quietly, 'but I can't lie to myself any longer. This rootless drifting is not for me.'

'What has come over you?' Shankhini broke the uneasy silence that had descended. 'Are you ill? Or in some trouble? Come, open your heart to me.'

'I'm not the Raja saheb you knew. I'm a different man.'

Shankhini burst out laughing, 'Don't worry. I have a cure for your ills.'

'What cure?'

'I've learned the black art from a tantric sanyasi.' Peal after peal of merry laughter rang like bells from Shankhini's lips as she continued, 'I can change you to what you were with a handful of magic dust. Come to my boat tonight. We'll dine together. And we'll talk. I have so much to say to you ... my heart brims over with ten years of unspoken words.'

*

Thoughts of Raja saheb kept Shankhini occupied for the rest of the day. What a fine figure of a man he had been in the past! His heart, mind and body intrepid and unflinching as though made of steel. The world had been his for the taking. She remembered the time he had murdered twelve men, buried their corpses on a bank of the Kaldighi, and returned with one hundred rupees tucked in his waistband and a smile on his lips. That blood had cooled. The same heart yearned to put down roots. For a quiet peaceful life. Alas! Shankhini knew no charms that could change him back to the man she had known and loved.

It wasn't as though she, herself, was not lured by the prospect of putting down roots. As though she wasn't consumed with envy at the sight of a woman flaunting the badge of wifehood. Didn't she drape a sari around her form, in secret, and fill her parting with sindoor? But she couldn't give up the power and privilege of being the queen of a band. She wanted Raja saheb as her husband but was not prepared to pay the price he wanted. She had to do something to bring the simmer back into his blood. To revive the old ruthlessness and lust for power. But she didn't know how…

Raja saheb is coming. Raja saheb is coming. A thousand bees hummed in Shankhini's heart. Looking out of the window of her hajarmoni boat she felt her senses sway in harmony with the lapping water. The sun was about to set. A cloud of red gold dust was clinging to reeds and bamboo clumps, tussock and broom. Suddenly she felt a wave of love for everything around her. For the changing hues of the sky. For the emerald-tailed kingfisher sitting on the arjun tree. For her own sensuous body. Music welled up in her throat and she sang…

Shaap-er bishe jemun temun; prem-er bishe du gun dhai
Gourango bhujango hoye dangshiyachhe amaar gaye
Bish-er jwala jemun jwala; prem er jwalai aagun dhai…

Snake poison is but little; love's poison is twice cursed
The fair one, turned serpent, has lashed my limbs and heart.
Snake poison may sting; love's poison is a flame…

Shankhini rose. Scrubbing her face with fuller's earth she washed it clean. She smoothed her cloud of unruly hair with fragrant oil and stuck a green beetle's wing between her brows. 'Palanki!' she called, her voice ringing with delight. '*O re O,*

Palanki! Come here. Come quick, you foolish girl. Braid my hair and put it up in a khonpa.'

Hurrying to Shankhini's boat, Palanka combed out the long, tangled hair with a wooden comb then, braiding it in seven strands, twisted it in an elegant coiffure. She watched wide-eyed as the older girl lined her eyes with surma, drew a pattern on her forehead with sandal paste and tucked a cluster of scarlet mandar flowers behind one ear. Clothes and ornaments came next. Securing her heavy breasts with a green-and-gold kanchuli, she hung a long skirt of saffron silk from her slim waist.

Shankhini had spent all afternoon weaving a chain of diamond teeth plucked from the jaws of a shankhamoni snake. This she wore around her neck. A topaz flower glimmered from one nostril and bunches of blood-red stones hung from her earlobes. Her wrists were heavy with mirror-shard bangles and a band of kanchuli bones rippled over her rounded hips. On her feet, brass anklets jingled and jangled. Her shapely body dazzled and glittered, with every movement, like shafts of lightning.

Palanka was gazing at Shankhini with awe in her eyes. The snake maiden had turned into a being from another world. She was as beautiful as the apsara Tilottama.

'*Ki lo*!' Shankhini smiled. Palanka's unconcealed admiration pleased her. 'Do you like the way I look?'

'Hunh.' Palanka answered in a dazed voice.

'Oh! my little bird … you like me … do you want to marry me?' Bursting into a peal of brazen laughter, she added, 'The trouble is you can't marry me even if you wish. I'm a woman.'

Palanka hung her head and was silent.

'You want to turn yourself into a wife … don't you, little bird? To build a nest of your own?'

Palanka raised her eyes and shot a timid glance at her mistress. A faint sound, which might have been an affirmative, escaped her lips.

At any other time, Shankhini would have snarled with fury at this admission. She would have threatened the girl with severe punishment. Even death. But this green-and-gold evening was magical. It was meant for joy and laughter. She blew an indulgent kiss at Palanka.

'Listen, Palanki,' Shankhini broke the silence that had fallen between them, 'I know you dress like a bride in secret. You think no one is looking. But I've seen you. You look so pretty that sometimes I wish I could marry you. But beware. My lover is coming tonight. Don't dare cast your eyes on him. If I catch you even...'

Shankhini stopped short. As suddenly as if she felt the forked tongue of a takshak lash her mouth. She was alarmed. *Why had she uttered those words? Did she feel threatened by the lovely young girl?* Her face hardened. Her indulgent tone became severe. 'Go,' she commanded, 'get out of this boat.'

Shocked at Shankhini's change of mood, Palanka hastened to obey.

The glimmering twilight faded. Dusk started to fall. Silhouetted against a sapphire-and-amethyst sky, a stream of ocean birds flew slowly towards the horizon. Shankhini stood by the window of her hajarmoni boat, waiting for her lover, as the shadows of night closed around Sonai Bibi-r Bil and the sound of rushing wings filled her air...

Mohabbat and the others had lit a fire on the bank into whose leaping flames they were throwing masses of waterbirds they had brought down with their harpoons earlier in the evening. Jalpipi, bakhari, dahuk and balihans. The flesh of these birds was plump and juicy.

Ha la la la! Ha la la la! Bedeys and bedeynis yelled in excitement. *Hui dhinak dhin! Hui dhinak dhin!* Some danced around the fire while others played drums and flutes. Zulfikar looked on with bloodshot eyes. In his arms, clutched with protective care, he held a dozen bottles of heady wine. Raja saheb was coming tonight and Shankhini was holding a feast in his honour. What could be a happier prospect? The drums beat harder and harder as the night advanced; the tunes from the flutes grew wilder. A drunken voice laden with nostalgia sang … *Kemon koira thaki lo soi Shyam-er bihaney.* An icy wind blew in gusts. But no one felt its bite. *Ha la la la! Ha la la la!* The night sky rang with intoxicated voices.

The long wait was over at last. At the sound of Raja saheb's footsteps, Shankhini moved from the window and glanced at herself in the mirror. A deep blush rose from her neck and stained her cheeks. Her glowing eyes grew misty. A tremendous happiness surged through her limbs like the waving waters of the fen. Stepping out of the boat, she walked towards her guest and took his large cool hands in her small fevered ones. 'Come in, Raja saheb,' she whispered. 'It's terribly cold outside…'

Hand in hand they walked into Shankhini's hajarmoni boat. After the biting chill of the bank, it felt warm and welcoming. A double-wicked lamp cast a soft orange glow on the two as they lay on a carpet, backs resting against silk cushions. Cuddling up to her lover, Shankhini whispered amorously, 'I've been looking out for you since evening. You took so long in coming. S-o-o-o long.' She waited for a reply and then, receiving none, she added fretfully, 'You don't love me anymore. Some wicked woman has ensnared you. Changed you. But don't forget that I'm Naagmati bedeyni's daughter, well versed in black magic. I know how to dispel the witch's charms and win you back. This night will be *our* night…'

At her words Raja saheb felt the old love of lust and power, bequeathed to him by generations of his nomadic ancestors, stir slowly in his blood. His eyes fell on the woman beside him. A snake maiden of incredible beauty! Sitting close ... so close her scent filled his nostrils. The warmth of her limbs pervaded his. An unknown mystique clung to her like a gossamer web. She was saying something but he couldn't hear a word. The clash of cymbals and the beat of drums from his own heart filled his ears. He turned to her with infinite tenderness and drew her to his breast.

'Ten years have gone by,' Shankhini whispered ruefully. 'Ten long years. If the storm hadn't separated us, if we were still in Asmani bedeyni's band, we could have been together for all time to come...'

Raja saheb had just opened his mouth to reply when Palanka walked in. Behind her were Aatarjaan, Gahar and Dohor Bibi. They carried wine bottles in their hands and clay pots full of different kinds of meat. There was khashi korma in one; roasted jalpipi in another. Imli bird curry, fried dahuk wings, juicy chunks of tender waterfowl cooked with garlic and spices, kanchuli snake kababs. So much variety! So many flavours! Dohor Bibi spread a piece of cloth on the carpet and arranged the pots with loving care.

Raja saheb's eyes wandered all over the deck. To the bunches of roots and herbs piled on one side and baskets, full of deadly snakes, on the other. It was a picture he had seen many times before, typical of the way bedeys lived. Suddenly, his roving eyes fell on Palanka who stood behind the other women. A sweet, pretty girl in a red striped sari and hijal flowers in her hair. There was something about her eyes that made him think of a humble cottage at dusk. His own grew misty with yearning. It was through this girl, he realized suddenly, that his dream could come true. In the quivering shadows of her gentle soul, he would find sanctuary…

Two women … Shankhini and Palanka. He looked from one to the other. Shankhini fired a man's blood, intoxicated him. Set his nerves on edge like a bow, strung taut. In Palanka he found a cool shadowy bower in which to rest them. Raja saheb's gaze grew soft; his heart melted with love. Shankhini was lightning. Palanka a humble flower.

'*Ei*, Palanki!' Shankhini's voice, like the sudden growl of a wounded tigress, shattered the silence. 'You whoring bitch! Get out of here. Get out this minute.'

Palanka had been gazing dreamily, all this while, at the man before her. She had read the message in his eyes and surrendered heart, mind and soul to him. Shankhini's harsh command broke into her reverie and she hastened to obey. But she was stopped. Putting out his hand, Raja saheb gripped hers. 'Why do you run away, dear?' He smiled at the girl. 'You've brought so much delicious food and wine. Stay and share some with us.'

'Let her go.' Shankhini laughed uneasily. 'She doesn't drink wine. And she has given up eating meat. The pretentious harlot has turned herself into a Boshtumi. Hee hee hee!'

'I too have given up wine…'

'What?' Shankhini couldn't believe her ears. Were they playing tricks with her? She sat dumbstruck for a few minutes, then burst into a peal of hyena-like laughter. 'Then you and the skinny myna-bird will make a wonderful pair. Boshtom and Boshtumi! Hee hee hee!'

Raja saheb was startled. Shankhini's laughter lashed at his eardrums like the deadly tongue of a hooded cobra and he released Palanka's hand. She hastened out of the boat with Dohor Bibi, Gahar and Aatarjaan close behind.

Hours passed. The winter night grew colder and darker. The wind shrieked and howled like the agonized cries of a soul in torment. The fire outside had burned down and the men and women sitting around it huddled together for warmth. Their excitement had waned by now. Heads were lolling on breasts and the thunderous voices that had set the heart of Sonai Bibi-r Bil quaking with fear were mute.

Shankhini moved closer to her lover and wound her arms around his neck. Her voice was drowsy with mahua fumes as she murmured dreamily, 'I can't live without you, Raja saheb. Be mine … only mine.'

'Do you really mean that?'

'I do. Ask me to swear on Allah or Bishohari … whoever you consider holier … and I'll obey.'

'If that's the way you truly feel,' Raja saheb sat up in excitement, 'let's build a home together. You've seen how village folk live. A deep bond of loyalty and faith binds couples till death parts them. The husband loves and protects his wife. She serves him, bears his children and raises them. Doesn't such a life appeal to you?'

'It does. But I love my life as a bedeyni even more. The danger and excitement of sailing over tumultuous waters, making snakes sway in rhythm to the tunes of my flute, preparing potions and working magic with poison stones … these things send a thrill through my bones and make my blood dance in ecstasy. We have been nomads for generations. A love of roving is in our blood. Don't even think of another way of life, Raja saheb. If you deny your heritage, you will invoke Bishohari's curse and all you hold dear will be destroyed. Be your old self again. Become the man you were when I saw you first.'

'I don't believe in Bishohari,' her companion said dismissively. 'I have wanted to give up this nomadic life for many years now. I haven't been able to ... so far. But I can't wait any longer. The time to renounce it has come.'

Shankhini froze at these words. She lay in her lover's embrace, limp and lifeless. She could scarcely breathe. She was a bedeyni, a devotee of Bishohari. Every muscle, tissue, cell and fibre of her being yearned for freedom. Freedom to sail her boat on uncharted waters. To weather storms and tempests. To feel the sun on her limbs and the wind on her face. Impossible for her to build a nest and stay confined within it. She couldn't do it. No ... not even for the man she loved.

Raja saheb stirred. 'It's time for me to go back,' he murmured, disengaging her arms gently. 'Goodbye, Shankhini.'

'But you haven't eaten anything!'

'I'm not hungry.'

'You're leaving!' A cry of pain escaped Shankhini's lips. 'One night! You refuse to be mine for even one night!' Tears clung to her eyelashes, like dewdrops on grass.

'You don't need me.'

'I need you. More than anyone or anything else. But what do *you* want from me?'

'You must leave the band. The bedeyni must turn herself into a farmer's wife.'

Shankhini was in a quandary. One half of her heart was drowned in love for Raja saheb. The tug of her roving blood and the rights and privileges she enjoyed as mistress of a band swamped the other. The two were mutually exclusive. She had to make a choice.

'Give me time to think,' she said. 'You'll come to my boat again, won't you?'

'Of course, I will. I've discovered another love here.' A low, mysterious laugh escaped Raja saheb's lips.

Shankhini shivered. An unknown fear took possession of her. She shut her eyes and tried to overcome it. There was something in Raja saheb's voice. An insinuation. What was it? She mulled over his words for a long time but couldn't fathom it.

She opened her eyes, after a while, to find him gone. She was alone. The boat was empty. As empty as her heart. She felt a bitter rush of bile in her throat. It corroded her mouth and set fire to her limbs. Suddenly a name rose to her lips. She spat into the food spread before her as she uttered it. *Palanka.* Every drop of her blood burned with hate. Her body swayed like a wounded snake with the pain of envy and thwarted love…

⋆

Raja saheb made his way carefully in and out of tussock clumps that stood as high as his chest. The merry chirping of crickets, alternating with the joyous croak of frogs from waterholes, came to his ears. Sonai Bibi-r Bil was wrapped in a shroud of dark mist. The only light came from clusters of glow-worms glittering, like sparks of emerald fire, from trees and bushes. The air was so cold it cut into his skin like a knife. He had a long way to go. He had to cross several streams and acres of kasharh jungle before he could reach his boat and find the comfort of a warm bed. He redoubled his pace.

Passing a piyal tree he stopped in his tracks. 'Raja saheb,' a soft voice had called out from the dark.

'Who is it?' He looked this way and that.

'I'm Palanka.' A slight figure slipped out of the shadows and stood before him. 'I've been waiting for you for hours.'

The light was so faint that he felt rather than saw the eyes fixed on his face. They were glowing like lamps. A pungent wild-flower scent, rising from her limbs, suffused his being.

Raja saheb felt as though he was in a dream. 'I knew I would find you again,' he murmured.

'I heard what you said to Shankhini.' Palanka came closer. 'I hid behind the boat and heard every word. I want a home too. A home and a husband. I'm tired of drifting from bank to bank. Will you take me away from here? We'll live like peasant folk do. Build a little hut and...'

'You'll come with me?' Raja saheb felt the blood leap joyfully in his veins. Before he realized what he was doing, he put out his arms and drew Palanka to his breast. Hours passed before Raja saheb released her. 'I must go now,' he said. 'The night is almost over.'

'You'll come again?' Palanka's voice throbbed with longing. 'When will I see you next?'

'Every day. I'll come to your band, every day.'

'*Un hunh*. Not to the band. Shankhini will be there. Come here again tomorrow. At dusk. I'll be waiting. If you fail me, I'll kill myself. I swear by Bishohari ... I will.'

Raja saheb gazed at her wild-flower face with love. The love, untouched by lust, he had kept hidden in his heart for the one who would be his soulmate. *She's a bedeyni*, he thought, *yet the blood runs pure and free in her veins. Untainted by the venom of her inheritance...*

'I'll come,' he said, 'if that's what you wish. I'll meet you here tomorrow.'

Raja saheb walked away. Palanka's heart felt as light as a bird's. Spreading her arms, like the wings of a dove, she flew through patches of light and shadow, over grass and water, towards the fleet of boats that belonged to Shankhini.

Next evening, in the green-gold dusk, Raja saheb met Palanka under the piyal tree. He came again the next day and the day after. Every evening. The scent of their love filled the air like fumes of heady wine.

'Come closer, bedeyni.' Raja saheb held out his arms. 'Come straight into my heart.'

'I am always in your heart, Raja saheb. But don't call me bedeyni. Call me *wife*,' Palanka whispered against his lips. 'When will you make me yours? I can't eat. I can't sleep. Like a love-sick bird I long for my mate.'

'A few more months. We'll leave after the rains. I'll marry you and take you away. Far away.'

'Where?'

'To Char Behula. Some farming folks are setting up a village there. We'll join them…'

'What will you do with your band? Your men, your boats, your snakes and weapons…?'

'I'll give them all to Shankhini. She loves me but she's unwilling to leave her band. It is more important to her than me. What can I do? Besides,' a shadow fell on Raja saheb's face, 'I'm taking you away from her. I must pay the price…'

'It is true that she loves you. Every evening, before I come here, I see her all dressed up waiting for you. She has begun to suspect me. She has set up spies everywhere. I have managed to evade them so far but only Bishohari knows with what difficulty! I'm afraid, Raja saheb. Mortally afraid. She'll kill me if she catches us together. She'll tear my limbs to shreds.'

'Why?'

'Why not? I have taken from her the man she loves. Can she forgive me?'

*

Another evening. Palanka stands under the lengthening shadows of the piyal tree locked in Raja saheb's arms. 'I can't bear being parted from you any longer,' she murmurs. Her tears fall on her lover's chest like a monsoon shower.

I can't bear being parted from you. Her own words accompanied by a screech of mocking laughter sizzles Palanka's ears as the lithe form of Shankhini slips from behind the piyal tree, where she had been hiding, and stands before her. '*Haramjadi*! Whoring wench!' she mutters between gritted teeth. Her mouth is twisted and ugly. Palanka's dream shatters into shards. Springing apart, the lovers stand like stone figures and stare at Shankhini with frozen eyes…

'Zulfikar!' Shankhini roars like a tigress whose cub has been snatched from her breast. The black mountain bulk of her right-hand man materializes from the shadows. His eyes sprout columns of fire like twin peaks of a volcano. His giant fists clench and unclench with fury.

'*Bajaan go*!' Palanka screams and buries her face deeper in Raja saheb's breast. Her frail body shivers like a leaf in a storm.

'*Bajaan go!*' Shankhini's voice, hissing like an adder's tongue, echoes through the trees. 'No Bajaan can save you from my clutches. *Haramjadi*! I dress up every evening and wait for my lover and you, you loathsome spawn of a worm, dare to lure him away? You've struck a cruel blow at my heart. I'll exact a terrible revenge. No, I shan't kill you. It would be too easy a death. I'll have vultures feed on your living limbs; gouge your eyes out with their beaks. *Oof!* So much venom lay concealed in your heart! I'll drain every drop of it out of your blood. I'll pull out your poisonous fangs from their roots. Take her away, Zulfikar. Take her to my boat and keep her tied to the mast till I come.'

The suddenness with which all this happened had left Raja saheb in such a state of shock that he looked on, paralysed, as Zulfikar flew at the girl like an enormous bird of prey and snatched her away from his breast. Minutes passed. The feral glare in Shankhini's eyes dimmed. Her heaving breast calmed and stilled. Her eyes turned dewy as she murmured in a honeyed voice, 'Raja saheb.'

Raja saheb turned to her. She looked dazzlingly beautiful in saffron silk and snake-bone ornaments. The statue came slowly to life. 'What is it?' he asked, his voice slurred as though still in a dream.

'Is Palanka more beautiful than me?'

'No.'

'Then why did you give her your heart? Be mine ... only mine.' Shankhini came close, so close, he could feel her breath, hot and moist, against his lips.

'I will be yours. But you must be mine first. You must come with me to Char Behula.'

Shankhini's limbs turned rigid. The colour left her face. 'But what about our bands?' she asked in a frightened voice. 'Our heritage, our livelihood, Bishohari ... won't her curse fall on us if we abandon them?'

'That's the trouble.' Raja saheb's voice was cold. Detached. 'You are a bedeyni to the core. You cannot be a wife. You'll never be able to leave your band...'

'Let me think about it. Give me a few days.'

'It's no use. You are not made for a humble life.' Raja saheb took her soft hands and gripped them in his own hard ones. 'Palanka is. Give her to me, Shankhini,' he begged.

Suddenly, something like a bolt of lightning struck the snake maiden's veins and, branching out in roots and shoots, struck her heart. She snatched her hands from Raja saheb's grip and ran out of the forest with the speed of a fleeing doe. Raja saheb looked on. A little smile flickered at the corner of his mouth.

*

A week went by. The rising sun continued to spread a soft, red-gold radiance across the sky. Mellow afternoons followed. Then, with day's end, a sad wan darkness fell like a mist over Sonai Bibi-r Bil.

That night, after Raja saheb begged her to give Palanka to him, Shankhini had fled like a hunted creature and, flinging herself on the deck of her hajarmoni boat, had broken into great shuddering sobs. Her lungs felt ripped and lacerated. Her heart burned with humiliation. Tears rained from her eyes, till there were none left. She was a bedeyni. She had been taught to endure the vagaries of nature. The assaults of the elements. Pain, sickness and fear. But she couldn't … she wouldn't endure defeat. Palanka's small wild-flower face came before her eyes. To think that *she* with her timid eyes and tiny-bird body had stolen her lover! That *she* was her rival! The thought was too painful to bear.

It was true that Raja saheb had started tiring of the life their kind had lived from time immemorial. He wanted to put down roots. But Shankhini could have stalled him. She knew she could. It was Palanka who had stirred his emotions and encouraged him to follow his heart. The wretched harlot had tempted him; had offered to be his wife. She had to be punished. Shankhini knew that the slightest gesture from her would send Zulfikar charging towards Palanka. He would twist her head from her body, as easily as plucking a flower from its stem, and bring it to her. He would scatter her torn limbs over Sonai Bibi-r Bil as lightly as dron petals. But Shankhini bided her time. For the present she kept the girl locked in a dim dark cabin in the boat that housed the panha ghar … a temple dedicated to Bishohari. Every band had a panha ghar in one of the boats. *Let the wretched creature spend a few days starving and pining for her lover*, she thought. She would think long and hard before deciding what to do with her.

Vengeance! What she needed was to wreak a terrible vengeance on the vassal who had betrayed her queen's deepest trust. The girl was unaware of what she had done. She had stretched her hand out towards the cruellest, fiercest of fires. Shankhini would make every inch of her flesh burn with mortification; every drop of her blood turn to liquid flame.

A few days later, Shankhini stood on the deck of her hajarmoni boat and called out to Zulfikar. It was a cold night. Dark and bitter, with a whistling wind. Instructions were given in sharp hissing tones.

An hour later the two stood outside the room in which Palanka had been confined. In his right hand Zulfikar held a metal rod the tip of which glowed with scarlet fire. In his other was a basin filled with coarse boiled rice. Shankhini unlocked the door. A lamp burned feebly in one corner. Palanka's naked body crouched close to it, arched like a bow, half-dead with cold.

'*Ei*!' Shankhini turned the girl over with her foot. 'Get up.'

Palanka rose to her feet. What followed was a volley of agonized screams as Zulfikar drew a line across her brow with the burning rod. Again and again, seven times, till it was furrowed with crimson streaks. '*Ki re!*' Peals of demonic laughter burst from Shankhini's lips. 'Will you try to snatch my lover from me again … spawn of a serpent? Will you? Answer me. Is your mouth still slavering for a home and a husband? With the marks I've drawn across your forehead you look like a Boshtumi beggar woman. Not even a whore.' Shankhini dropped down beside the weeping girl. 'I'll bring a mirror tomorrow,' she said, laughing. 'You can see your face for yourself. Do you think Raja saheb will bother to cast another glance at you? Tell me, little bird. Are you still in love with him?'

'Yes, I am.' Palanka raised her head and looked at her tormenter. Her eyes were still streaming but, with a fearlessness she hadn't even known she possessed, she added, 'And I'll continue to love him till I die. You've lost him because there is no love in your heart. No … not for anyone. All you can do is take out your frustrations on others.'

'*Arre arre!* The worm turns into a snake!' Shankhini's lips twisted with scorn. 'You haven't learned your lesson yet, I see. You need a little more teaching. Remember one thing. I'm the daughter of Naagmati bedeyni. I can root out every kind of venom. Be it snake or human.'

Leaving the rice on the floor, Zulfikar and Shankhini walked out of the room. Shankhini turned the key in the lock and looked at the sky, a dim sky streaked with mist. *How Palanka had changed*, she thought with a pang in her heart. *What was the source from which the broken bird was deriving her strength? Could it be Raja saheb's promise of a nest? What if she, Shankhini, followed her example? If she allowed her lover to lead her by the hand to a tiny hut in an obscure village by the bank of some distant river? If she turned herself into a loving wife and caring mother?*

*

Next morning three men arrived with a message from the leader of the Barui community of Bajitpur. A snake had bitten a worker in his betel grove and Shankhini's expertise was required to save his life.

Shankhini made haste to obey the summons. One of the tenets of their faith was rushing in answer to such a call. It was Bishohari's implicit command. With a bag full of poison stones slung from one shoulder, a basket of roots and herbs on her head and an earthen plate in her hands, Shankhini came to the panha ghar. Dohor Bibi accompanied her. Before venturing on an important task, members of her band came here to pay obeisance to Bishohari and seek her blessings. A clay image of the goddess they had moulded themselves was set atop a coil of seven snakes. The giant hood of a kaliya naag formed an umbrella above her head. An udai naag hung from her neck like a garland and a khoijati was her bracelet. A kanchuli formed from the intertwining bodies of a chakrachud and a shankha naag covered her voluptuous breasts. Takshak and laudaga wove themselves into a skirt for her lower limbs and shuto shankha, thread-snakes, wound themselves into rings for her fingers. A couple of deadly danrash were her anklets and swinging merrily from her ears were the fanned-out hoods of white sada chiti. Incense burning in a censer filled the room with fragrant smoke.

Shankhini prostrated herself and touched the ground with her forehead. Her hands were folded in a humble plea. Drawing out snake venom was arduous; even dangerous. She could do it, she had done it often, but she needed the goddess's blessing. She shot a glance at the image. And what she saw shocked her. The tender love that irradiated Bishohari's face had vanished. A stern, cruel gleam had replaced the benign light in her eyes. Even the snakes around her coiled and uncoiled their bodies in agitation, fanned their hoods and spat venom from angry tongues. The air was full of hissing sounds. The incense burning before the image gave out clouds of evil-smelling smoke. Shankhini's limbs grew numb. Her senses swam. The blood running in her veins stood still.

'Make haste, Amma,' Dohor Bibi's voice came to her ears, as though from a vast distance. 'We are very late as it is. Who knows what we'll find on reaching Bajitpur.'

Shankhini shut her eyes and ran out of the panha ghar. She dared not stay there any longer. *Any moment now*, she thought with dread in her heart, *the snakes will come streaking out like meteors and crawl over me. They'll lash my face with their hoods and dig their fangs into my limbs.* Sweat ran down her body like rain. In her heart was the roll of distant drums. She realized the truth. Bishohari had turned away from her; had taken away the right to utter incantations in her name. Shankhini had lost her power. A scream, trapped in her chest, did not reach her lips…

Meanwhile, the men from Bajitpur were getting restless. 'Make haste, bedeyni,' they said. 'We have a long way to go.'

Shankhini was in a quandary. She couldn't refuse to go with them. It would mean disobeying Bishohari's express command. She had to shed all her misgivings and rush to save a victim of snake bite. But could she do so without the goddess's benediction? As though in a dream Shankhini followed the men, Dohor Bibi walking by her side, into the wilderness of thorn, tussock, screw pine and bulrush, till they reached the piyal tree. Here her footsteps stopped. Her eyes widened with horror. For what she beheld was another world. A world one entered only after death…

She had been trying all this while to compose herself. To clear her mind of doubts and fears. To concentrate on the incantations that would enable her to do her task. But the figure waiting under the piyal tree, as though on a lover's tryst, drove everything out of her head. Raja saheb's large dark eyes pierced into hers; held them with an unflinching gaze.

'Where is Palanka?' he asked her, 'I haven't seen her for many days.'

The anger and frustration she had been trying to subdue all this while came gushing out of Shankhini like steam from a boiling kettle. Her fears vanished. Her listless spirit sprang to active life as though lit with a blazing torch. 'Palanka is in her grave,' she muttered through clenched teeth. 'Listen, Raja saheb. You cannot stay here any longer. I'm on my way to

Bajitpur. I wish to see the fen cleared of you and your band on my return.' She walked away without a backward glance. But, no matter how hard she tried to dispel it, a thought kept tearing at her heart. Torturing her. *Did she really want Raja saheb to leave Sonai Bibi-r Bil? If so, why had she entreated him to stay that first day? Why?*

Shankhini returned two days later, her limbs burning with fever, her eyes the flaming red of hibiscus flowers. Her hair was a tangled nest and her clothes soiled and dishevelled. Like one possessed she ran to the panha ghar and threw herself on the floor at Bishohari's feet.

⋆

It was late afternoon. The sun's rays, hard and glittering like mica, enveloped the earth in white-hot light. The members of Shankhini's band stood waiting outside the panha ghar. A little distance away Dohor Bibi stood weeping and trembling. All eyes turned to her. '*Ki lo*, Dohor!' Mohabbat muttered uneasily. 'You went with her to Bajitpur. What happened there? I don't understand...'

Dohor Bibi threw a fearful glance in the direction of the woman in the panha ghar. Shankhini lay curled, like a snail afraid to come out of its shell. Her body shuddered with sobs. Tears streamed out of her eyes in an unstoppable flood. 'Bishohari's curse has fallen on her,' Dohor Bibi answered. 'She was unable to utter a single mantra. She was speechless, unmoving, like a block of stone. She just sat by the boy's side and watched him die.'

The faces around her turned pale. Eyes popped out of their sockets. 'Bishohari appeared to her in a dream,' Dohor continued. 'I heard her pacing up and down the room, all night, weeping as if her heart would break. By morning her body was shaking with a raging fever. Her eyes were fire-red. She ran all the way here, swaying and staggering like a drunken woman. I tried to stop her but she wouldn't listen to a word. What could I do? I ran after her as fast as I could.'

Shankhini lay on the floor of the panha ghar all through the day, so still ... life seemed to have left her limbs. Then, with the falling dusk, she rose to her feet. She had spent her tears. Her eyes burned like smouldering coals. But her mind was clear. She knew that she had committed a grievous sin and Bishohari had meted out a terrible punishment. She had taken away her powers. For the first time in her life Shankhini saw herself for what she truly was. A cruel, thwarted woman in the throes of an unrequited love. She realized that Raja saheb was a distant star she could never hope to reach. She had thought she could, through force of will. But it was only an illusion.

Outside, in the darkening forest, a pair of jackals were yelping love calls to one another. Between them, they sent eddies of sound across stretches of reeds and humps of earth that rose from the shallow water. Dohor Bibi, Moina and Aatarjaan sat outside the panha ghar with Shankhini in their midst. She had ripped off her skirt and kanchuli. They lay by her side in a discarded heap. Her jewels she had flung all over the floor. The snake maiden's nude body lay coiled like a golden snake, in hibernating slumber.

Presently she rose. Taking up an enormous censer of burned clay in both hands she commenced waving clouds of incense smoke before the image of Bishohari. Dancing and genuflecting she offered obeisance. She had sinned. She had allowed herself to stray from the path laid down by the goddess. She had put her love of a mortal above that of the divine. She had desired her lover with so much passion that she hadn't stopped to reflect on the cost. Stripping oneself in body before the goddess, surrendering all thought and feeling at her feet, was the way bedeynis had atoned for their sins from time immemorial.

The dancing went on through the night. Smoke from the censer clouded the room. The air in the panha ghar turned opaque and acrid. Then, with the first pearling of the east, Shankhini fell to the floor in a dead faint. The censer crashed and broke into shards. Pieces of burning husk flew about the room and dropped on her motionless form, scorching the silk-smooth skin, blistering it.

Her eyes opened to a flame of the forest dawn turning to liquid gold. She sat up. A deep peace, such as she had never known before, pervaded her being. She lifted her face to the sky and sang:

It is at Her bidding that the sun rises from the east.
Lakhai wakes from the dead, sits in his boat and smiles.
Ah me! So great is Bishohari's mercy…

The sound of footsteps brought her out of her trance. Raja saheb stood before her. She felt the blood leap and whirl in her veins. A hundred joyous chords jangled in her ears. But only for a minute. Then her pulse fell into a gentle rhythm and her heart was still and tranquil.

'We would have left the fen just as you wished,' Raja saheb said. 'Only…'

'I know what kept you,' Shankhini stopped him in mid-sentence. She felt a strange disconnect. As though she was speaking to a stranger. As though there had never been anything between them. 'You've come to ask me for Palanki.'

'Yes,' Raja saheb exclaimed, his voice eager. 'Let me have her. I'll give you everything I possess in return. My band, my boats…'

'I don't want anything. Except to be relieved of the burden I carry. The girl who never ceases to remind me of you. Take her away from here. Save me from Bishohari's wrath. Only promise me one thing. That you two will never come into my presence again.'

'Do you really mean it? Do you? Swear on my head…' He moved towards her.

'Don't come near me.' She shrank involuntarily from his touch. 'You smell different. Of home and hearth. Go to Palanki. Tell her you'll marry her tomorrow. I'll make all the arrangements.' Seeing his bewildered eyes fixed on hers, she added, 'Don't worry. I'll keep my word. A bedeyni does not lie.'

Raja saheb stood transfixed for a few moments. Then, turning, he fled as though on wings into the forest. Shankhini watched him go. Waves of pain lashed against her heart but she subdued them. Never again would she allow herself to weaken; to go against the laws framed by her ancestors.

*

Raja saheb and Palanka stood on either side of a waterhole the bedeys had dug earlier that day. A muga curtain separated them. Surrounding them in a ring were men and women from both bands. The bride's petite form was wrapped in deep red silk. Sandalwood etchings marked her brow. A garland of white lotus buds swung gently on her breast and tooth jewels glittered from her neck and arms. Raja saheb was equally resplendent in a kingfisher-blue silk lungi with peacock feathers waving from his raven locks. The two faces glowed in the amber-gold light of the setting sun. From the deck of her hajarmoni boat, Shankhini watched the scene.

Homra bedey from Bhataar Mari-r Bil had been invited to perform the ceremony. His hair was the colour of straw, his eyes fogged with liquor fumes, and his skin so dry, it seemed to flake with every movement. A bow was fitted at his waist and a quiver of plumed arrows hung from one shoulder. Puffing out his stomach with self-importance he said, 'The moment of *Shanazar*, the auspicious exchange of glances, has arrived. Are the bride and bridegroom willing?' Raja saheb swayed his head solemnly and Palanka trembled in response. Homra bedey lifted the curtain and the lovers saw each other's face reflected in the clear water.

'The nuptial ceremony is over,' Homra announced. 'The couple are married.'

A volley of delighted exclamations accompanied by bursts of song rose from the crowd. Sonai Bibi-r Bil shared their joy. Her trees swayed from side to side and her leaves and grass rippled with delight.

Shankhini covered her ears and ran into the panha ghar. She sat, for hours afterwards, gazing at the goddess. Imploring her to take away her pain…

Outside, around a glowing fire, members of both bands were celebrating. Dozens of empty bottles rolled about on the bank. The sky reverberated with drumbeats and the music of flutes grew wilder with every passing hour. The heart of Sonai Bibi-r Bil rumbled with an ecstasy akin to fear.

The bride and bridegroom sat in a vast grass boat, surrounded by bedeynis in motley-coloured skirts and kanchulis. The smiles on their faces glittered sharp as knives. Lightning darted from kohl-lined eyes. Each was wrapped in a dream. A beautiful dream that had seemed unreal, unachievable, so far, but was no longer so.

Shankhini walked out of the panha ghar towards the group. Her eyes were fixed on Raja saheb as he sat among the women.

Shafts of light flashed from his form as though from the petals of a diamond lotus. There was something strange about him. Unreal. As though he had appeared to her in a vision. Currents of illicit passion ran through her blood. All the vows she had made to the goddess receded. Bishohari's warnings disappeared like lines drawn on water. 'Listen, Palanki,' she whispered feverishly in the girl's ears, 'come out for a moment. I have something to say to you.'

Shankhini's breath, hot and stormy, blew in the girl's face as they stood on the bank facing each other. Her eyes glittered like pieces of burning glass. Her limbs quivered as though snakes were wriggling in her blood stream.

'What is it, Amma?' Palanka's voice was a frightened whisper.

'I'll give you my boats, my band, my jewels ... everything I have. All I want in return is Raja saheb. Give him to me.'

'No. Never.' Palanka covered her ears and ran towards the boat. 'I can't. I can't.'

Shankhini stared at the retreating form. 'You think you'll lie in my lover's arms tonight, don't you?' she muttered out of clenched teeth. 'Be prepared for a shock.' She strode into the forest, determination stamped on every line of her face. She needed something. She had to find it before it was too late...

An important ritual of a Hindu marriage is the exchange of floral garlands by the bride and bridegroom. It is called *mala badal*. The snake-charming community from the river-swamps of Bengal follow a similar custom. The only difference is that what the couple hang on each other's necks are living snakes. Snakes that have been tamed and defanged and, in consequence, harmless.

The night turned dense and dark. And now the women who had been humming like bees around the bride and bridegroom sat up. 'It's late,' Aatarjaan said, yawning. 'Time for the mala badal. Bring the snakes, Dohor.'

'I've brought them.' Shankhini appeared suddenly in their midst, a basket balanced on each shoulder. 'I'm the queen of this band. It is for me to do the honours.' The women noticed the secretive smile on her lips and the two tiny flames that flickered from the pupils of her eyes. They stared at one another in horror but no one had the courage to utter a word.

'Come, Raja saheb. Come, my little blackbird.' She held out a basket to each. 'Take out the snakes and garland each other. The bridegroom, first, as is the custom.'

A shudder passed over Palanka's frame. Something was amiss. She was sure of it. But what could it be? She glanced fearfully at her mistress. Raja saheb appeared unfazed. His lips parted in a pleased smile as he took the basket from Shankhini's hand. But the moment he pried open the lid the smile vanished. For, what shot up from the depths of the basket was an enormous kalchita, caught fresh from keya clumps growing in the heart of the fen. Swift as a blazing meteor, it stood on its tail hissing viciously, then, with a dart of its fanned hood, dug its fangs into Raja saheb's brow. Two drops of blood, like glittering rubies, appeared on the golden skin as Raja saheb's body swayed and fell to the floor. Palanka stood, as though paralysed, watching her husband's limbs turning blue from the deadly poison. Her throat was choked. She could neither speak nor weep. An eerie silence fell on the wedding party.

It was broken by a peal of cruel laughter that tinkled like breaking glass. '*Ki lo*, Palanki!' Shankhini mocked the hapless girl. 'You wanted to take my lover from me, didn't you? Take him. He is all yours. Embrace him. Enjoy his kisses.'

A moment later she threw herself at Raja saheb's prostrate form with a bloodcurdling scream. 'What have I done? *Ma go!* What have I done?' She leaned over him and shook him violently. But the man she was so desperately trying to bring back to life lay motionless in her arms. She rose to her feet and looked this way and that, her eyes blank. *The venom of Kalchita isn't so swift to act*, she thought wonderingly, *then why did Raja saheb succumb to it so quickly? Was the poison the reptile spewed in Raja saheb's veins not its own? Was it mine? Was it I who gathered all the venom, that burned like fire in my heart and soul, and thrust it under the kalchita's tongue? Was it I who turned myself into the fanned hood of the creature I caught from the depths of the fen? Were those my deadly fangs that lashed my beloved's brow?*

Wave after wave of guilt and bitter regret passed over her as her body became as cold and lifeless as the one which lay at her feet.

Illegal Immigrant

Nakul Mallik

The local train from Bongaon to Canning came and went as it pleased. Yet Madhab always made it a point to reach the station well before the appointed time. He went to the factory first, of course, to pick up his stuff. Filling the barrel given to him with fresh puffed rice, he put a pot of burning coal on top to keep it warm. Next, he chopped onions, cucumber, green chillies and coriander and filled the little brass bowls set around the rim. Once inside the train, there was no time for anything other than moving from compartment to compartment jingling the brass bells around his wrist. A sound that invited passengers to buy Madhab's famous spiced jhal muri.

Very often he didn't go all the way to Canning. He would get off at some other station … Sonarpur or Kalikapur, and make his way to the local bazar, school or college. Sometimes he even set up his barrel outside the court premises. He was so well known in these places that he didn't even need to call out to anyone. The jingling of his bells was enough to attract customers.

No matter how late it got, Madhab didn't go home till he had sold all the jhal muri in his barrel. He could be seen darting from this bench to that of the Canning Local, making up paper cones of the mouth-watering stuff, handing them to his customers and counting the money he received, till the moon was halfway up in the sky. The train ferried passengers till midnight.

After selling his entire stock he made his way to the factory, returned the empty barrel and gave the owner his share of the profits. Reaching home, he ate the rice and dal his wife had cooked at dusk. Though ice cold by the time he sat down to his meal, he ate with relish and got ready for bed just as Shefali had risen from it. It was at this precise hour, when the sky was pearling with first light, that she began getting ready to catch the train to Kolkata with her basket of flowers, garlands, tulsi and bel leaves. Husband and wife saw each other for a few minutes with just enough time to exchange a few pleasantries.

Madhab's father had taken refuge in India while the war of liberation was being fought. After Bangladesh became independent, he had answered the call of his roots and gone back to his native village with his wife and children. But to his surprise he had found that the new country was very different from the one he had left behind. The poverty and deprivation the family had to face was so acute, starvation and semi-starvation became the norm. They had struggled for a few years, then, like so many others, were forced to return. Once back, unable to cope with the reality of his situation, Madhab's father turned himself into an invalid. In consequence, the burden of maintaining his old parents and younger siblings fell on the eldest boy Madhab's young shoulders. Fortunately, his sister had been married off by then so there was one mouth less to feed.

At first Madhab went from town to town, from Chakda to Bhaina, from Bhaina to Bagula, trying to find shelter with one or other of his relatives. Then, drawing a blank everywhere, he built a small leaf hut in a refugee slum at the edge of the Bongaon line, and started selling jhal muri. This was nearly ten years ago. His parents had died since then and his siblings had branched out on their own. He had led a solitary existence for several years, then, only last year, he had found a companion in Shefali.

Their hut had such a low ceiling that they could only sit or lie down in it. They couldn't stand without endangering their skulls. The walls were so thin, the faintest whisper from the adjoining hut could be heard. It had no proper door. The interior was clearly visible to the people outside. Madhab and Shefali lived in constant fear of their few possessions being stolen.

But that wasn't their only fear. Jackals and wild dogs would wander in and out of the slum and steal chickens and ducks. During the monsoon months, strong winds and rain would lash against the frail huts, threatening to pull them down. There were other worries. Some news or other kept the slum dwellers awake every night. A rumour had surfaced lately that all Bangladeshis who had come to India after 1971 were to be deported. The Central government had designated them as *Illegal Immigrants*. They had entered the country without the requisite documents and were putting a strain on its resources. India was struggling with a population explosion of its own. Why should she shoulder the additional burden of encroaching Bangladeshis?

At first, Madhab turned a deaf ear to these rumours. Engaged from morning till night in making a living, he had no time for news-mongering and speculation. Shefali had no fears at all. She was not a Bangladeshi. She had been born in India, in a small village called Subuddhipur that lay to the west of Baruipur. Her family belonged to the farming community though they owned no land. Her father had made a precarious living by working in other people's fields and could rarely give his family two square meals a day. Shefali had faced many years of hardship before finding a husband as energetic and hardworking as Madhab. Now she was content. She didn't allow other fears to worry her.

Things had got so bad some years ago that she was forced to think of ways to augment her father's meagre income. One of their neighbours, a friendly widow she addressed as Boudi, elder brother's wife, used to catch the first train to Kolkata every morning with a basket of flowers, garlands, bel and tulsi leaves which she sold in the city markets. Shefali decided to follow her example. This was the only business that could be run with practically no capital. Her father, grateful for whatever little money she brought home each day, did not stop her. And over the years he became dependent on her earnings. As a result, each day became a nightmare for the poor girl. All hopes of a normal life with a husband and children became a distant dream. Acutely unhappy and dispirited, she struggled on.

Then, when she had reached the deepest depths of despair, she met Madhab.

Shefali was a shy, timid girl but, with the passing of time, she developed confidence. She became smart and clever. She started moving all over the city and sold her wares after expert haggling. One late afternoon, on her way back home with her boudi, the train stopped a few miles away from Bagha Jatin station. Hours went by but it wouldn't budge. From the conversation of their fellow passengers, they gathered that there was an electrical breakdown somewhere. It was being attended to but who knew when the train would start again?

Shefali's stomach rumbled with hunger. But where in the middle of waving rice fields would they find food? The other passengers had already bought up everything the hawkers in the train were selling. She lay with her head in Boudi's lap, famished and exhausted, eyes staring at the view outside.

A jhal muri seller was sitting a little distance away from them. Boudi beckoned to him. 'Do you have anything left in your barrel?' she asked without much hope. But the man rose instantly and hastened towards them. 'I have some left at the bottom, Didi. How much do you want?'

'My sister-in-law is dying of hunger. She'll need a whole barrelful.' Boudi burst out laughing. So did Shefali. She looked askance at the jhal muri seller. He was smiling benignly at her. '*Achha achha*,' he said comfortably. 'Eat your fill. Go on eating till the barrel is empty.' He blew a few puffs at the pot of smouldering coal. Then, filling a large tin, he tossed the warmed mixture up and down, making the bells at his wrist jingle merrily.

'I cannot pay much,' Shefali whispered to Boudi.

'You don't have to pay anything,' the muri seller answered for Boudi. 'Eat as much as you want.'

That was their first meeting. There were many more after that. Madhab started making it a point to be on the train Shefali caught every afternoon on her way home. And, at some time or other, he would make his way to the compartment in which she and Boudi were sitting. Shefali waited in eager anticipation, ears cocked, for the jingling of bells that announced his approach.

Madhab came, chatted for a while, gave her a large cone of the mixture, but waived away the money she offered. Shefali felt embarrassed, especially when this happened in the presence of other girls who travelled on the same train and had become her friends. They teased her and asked, 'How long will you two carry on like this?' Boudi also observed what was going on and decided to do something about it. She invited Shefali to her house for lunch on the day of the Bengal Bandh and, after some gossip about this and that, brought up the subject of the jhal muri seller.

'Have you found out anything about him?' she asked.

'He's unmarried,' Shefali replied, eyes on the ground, nervous fingers pulling a flower from Boudi's basket to pieces. 'He has no parents and lives by himself in the slum by the side of the railway line in Bongaon. He's a Bangladeshi.'

'What difference does that make?' Boudi smiled at her.

'He lives in a tiny leaf hut...'

'That shouldn't be a problem.' Boudi giggled. 'As long as it can accommodate a man and a woman...'

It was Boudi who did all that was needed to be done. Sending for Madhab, she introduced him to Shefali's parents and obtained their consent.

Shefali came to Madhab's hut and made it her home. She had seen poverty and struggle, had known hunger and privation, but what she saw around her, now, was too bitter for words. The ceiling of their hut was so low, she couldn't stand straight without hitting her head. There was no veranda. The door was so flimsy, it served practically no purpose.

No welcoming ululation or blowing of conch-shells greeted the new bride. There was no one to bless her with durba grass and paddy. Even the mandatory phoolsajja ceremony, the ritual that entitled bride and bridegroom to sleep together, was not performed. Spreading flowers on a mat spread on the damp earth that was their floor, seemed a travesty. The hut was so close to the railway line that they got a clear view of the passengers sitting in the trains that ran day and night. And every time a train passed, the hut shivered and shook so violently that the rice pot on the kitchen fire jumped up and down. The noise was so loud sometimes that Shefali was rudely jerked from sleep. For the first time she realized what it was to be a refugee in another country.

The early days were difficult. She had never lived in such close proximity with so many people and couldn't bear the curious stares of her neighbours. Tears would gush into her eyes at the slightest provocation. 'All will be well dear,' Madhab would say lovingly, taking her in his arms. 'This is the way people in this slum have lived for years. We are all refugees; all in the same boat. It is a matter of habit. You'll get used to it in time. But don't despair. You won't have to stay here forever. I have my eye on a hundred yards of land, a little distance away, and some money put by already. The rest we will save from our joint earnings. It will take us about a year to buy the land and build our own hut.'

Shefali would listen to his words of comfort without much hope. She had to keep reminding herself that she had married him because she loved him and had to be content with her lot. She had no alternative.

After a few days, life fell into a pattern. She started going out again with her basket. This time she found a companion in one of her neighbours. They bought flowers from Thakurnagar, on their way back home, and spent the evening stringing them into garlands. Then, at early dawn next day, they caught the train to Kolkata.

Madhab woke up much later and cooked a meal. He put by a generous amount for her, taking care to cover the thala with a heavy vessel, safe from marauding cats and dogs. Then, after eating the rest, he went out to do his selling for the day. He returned at midnight, sometimes even later. Husband and wife had the briefest time together; a couple of hours at the most. Shefali got exasperated at times. What kind of life was this?

Where was the joy of union she had dreamed of? Husband and wife were denied even one whole night together. Except on the days that trains stopped running due to some disturbance. Then Madhab was the happiest of men. 'Freedom!' he exclaimed ecstatically. 'Absolute freedom! We'll spend the whole day making love.'

'What about the flowers I bought yesterday?' Shefali mumbled in pretended disappointment. 'They'll go waste. So much money gone down the drain.'

'They won't go waste,' Madhab put his arms around her and whispered in her ear. 'We'll scatter them on our mat tonight. We'll lie on a bed of flowers and dream lovely dreams.'

'Stop it.' Shefali burst into tears. 'What wasn't possible on the first night won't be possible ... ever again.'

Life went on. Struggle and stress, hard work and unfulfilled hopes didn't make a serious dent in their relationship. Despite occasional quarrels their days passed smoothly enough.

One day, as Madhab was hawking his wares, he heard a piece of news. It wasn't new. He had heard it, off and on, several times before. But today all the passengers in the train were discussing it with frenzied excitement. The government had decided that all encroachments by Bangladeshis, including slums that had stood for years, would be razed to the ground and the inmates forcibly deported to their own country. And it would happen soon; very soon.

For the first time Madhab was frightened. Truly frightened. He came home early that night but couldn't summon up the courage to share the news with Shefali. Shefali sensed something wrong. Madhab's face was pale and taut and he was unusually quiet. She had never seen her husband like this.

'What's wrong with you?' she asked worriedly. 'Are you feeling unwell?'

'No.'

'Then why do you look so grim?'

Madhab dodged her question with a few mumbled words.

He went out each day with his barrel of jhal muri but the old enthusiasm was gone. He did his day's work mechanically, ears cocked to hear what the babus in the train were discussing. He read newspapers, whenever he could get hold of them, painstakingly spelling out the words.

One morning, Sudhir, the candy seller, came close to him and whispered, 'Have you heard the news Madhab-da?'

'What news?'

'We'll have to go back to the village.'

Madhab's heart stopped beating and his limbs broke out in a sweat. The fear that had been gnawing at his chest like a mouse, for so many days, suddenly took on gigantic proportions. It became a tiger with deadly fangs. His mouth went dry and he stared with unseeing eyes at Sudhir.

Stepping off the train, Madhab tried to calm his mind and compose his features. He had to appear his normal self before Shefali. She was a perceptive woman, quick to sense a difference in her husband's face and manner. Lifting the empty barrel on his shoulder he walked with slow, measured steps towards the factory, paid the owner his share of the earnings and started walking home. On the way he heard a radio blaring the latest news from one of the shops. In some village or other, armed police had forcibly evicted some Bangladeshis from their homes and carried them away in trucks across the border.

Madhab dragged his feet back to his hut. His mind was numb and his limbs frozen with fear. Stumbling through the door he sank in a heap on the floor.

Next morning, he gathered the other inmates of the slum and shared the news. They would have to work out a strategy, he told them. What had happened to others today, might happen to them tomorrow. What would they do then?

A lot of ideas were put forward. But not one seemed practical or feasible. Fear and tension were writ large on all faces. Only Shefali seemed unconcerned. 'This is fake news,' she said to her husband. 'So many people live along the railway line. How can everyone be evicted? It's not possible.'

Madhab couldn't share her confidence. He formed a band with a few chosen men from the slum and went to meet the members of the local party in power. 'What you've heard is true,' they said after some deliberation. 'We've heard it too. But…'

'What will happen to us? Please think of something.'

'Yes, yes, something will have to be done of course. But…'

'But what, Babu?'

'The problem is that you are divided. You need to organize yourselves into a workforce.'

'How do we do that?'

'Do I have to spell it out?' The party chief's lips twisted in a smile. 'Get everyone in the slum together and start working for us. Only a strong political party can raise your issues in parliament.'

Disheartened, Madhab and his compatriots went to the chief of the other party. But what they heard was a parrot-like repetition. The ruling party was corrupt and would do nothing for them. Depending on those guys would be useless. The members of the opposition, on the other hand, were committed to the welfare of ordinary people. But they needed to have their hands strengthened. They wanted people like Madhab and other slum dwellers to work for them. How else would they be able to find a solution to their problem?

Madhab spent the next few days in visiting his relatives. From Chakda to Bagula, Ranaghat to Shantipur, everywhere he went, uncles, aunts, cousins and second cousins all expressed the same fears. Of being hounded out of the country where they had managed to make a living, however precarious, and being flung into one long left behind. Everyone had a story to tell. Some of these were true, some grossly exaggerated.

'I saw a truck carrying away our people,' one said. This seemed possible.

'Men, women and children were all crammed together like hens in a cage,' another offered his bit. 'The police pointed rifles at their heads and threatened to shoot them if they made a sound. Even babies in their mothers' arms were not spared.' This account didn't convince even the most susceptible of his listeners.

With all this running about, Madhab had stopped going out with his barrel of jhal muri. But Shefali went about her business as usual. She had no fears.

'Let's leave the slum,' Madhab said to Shefali more than once. 'Let's go to some place where no one knows I am a Bangladeshi. The police will pick me up, sooner or later, if I stay on here.'

'Nonsense,' Shefali snapped at him. 'So many people live in this slum. How many can they carry off to Bangladesh? It's easier said than done. Besides, who's afraid of the police? Let them try to lay a finger on you. Don't I have my broomstick ready to lash about their heads? Stop worrying.'

A month went by. Shefali went about her business as usual. She took the first train to Kolkata every morning, sold her flowers, and returned by the afternoon one. But Madhab's anxiety would not ease. He went to work one day and stayed home the next. The nagging fear that Sudhir's words had set off in his mind gnawed and nibbled at it day and night.

It was a Tuesday. Shefali stepped off the train in the late afternoon to sense something odd in the air. The platform was deserted for the most part. Only a few people, huddling together in a knot, were speaking in agitated whispers. Shefali's heart missed a beat. Her sixth sense told her that something was wrong.

She turned her steps towards the slum. As she walked, she noticed an absence of the hustle and bustle that was usual at this hour on other days. An unnatural calm pervaded the atmosphere. The lane was deserted. Only a few men could be seen standing in twos and threes, here and there. They averted their eyes at her approach. Shefali's heart sank and her legs felt as heavy as lead but she willed herself to walk on. The bag, containing a few vegetables and a coconut she had bought from the bazar in Kolkata, pressed into her shoulder like a deadweight. Reaching the slum, she called out to the neighbouring children who usually played outside at this hour, 'Radhu! Kalu! Madhu!' Then, receiving no response, she called out to their mother, '*Ki go*, Baisakhi-r Ma? Where are you? And where are your little ones?'

A death-like quiet met her words.

Stepping into her yard Shefali got the shock of her life. All her household articles … clothes, kanthas, mats, pillows and cooking vessels lay scattered here and there. A broken pail rolled drunkenly in a corner. There was no sign of her husband.

'*Koi go!*' she cried out in panic. 'What's going on? Where are you?'

No response.

'Are you out?' she tried again.

Terror-stricken, she ran to her neighbour's hut. '*O go, ki hobe go!* she wailed. 'O Nayantara-r Ma, where are you? And where are all the others?' The empty room and eerie silence struck her heart with a deathly chill. She couldn't breathe. Even the wind, it seemed to her, had stopped blowing.

She realized that the inmates of the slum had been spirited away somewhere and only their abandoned huts remained. She looked on with glazed eyes as a mangy old dog crept out of her neighbour's kitchen. It was slavering at the mouth and grains of rice were dripping from it.

She walked towards the railway line where a crowd had gathered. Seeing her bewildered look, an old gentleman came towards her and said, 'The police were here last night. They carried everyone away even as they lay sleeping.'

'Why?' An agonized shriek burst from Shefali's throat.

The man looked at her with lacklustre eyes. 'They were illegal immigrants. They're being sent back to Bangladesh.'

Shefali threw herself on the ground weeping. Knocking her head against it, over and over again, she screamed and hurled curses at the police. Then, rising with a sudden movement, she pulled herself together. 'Do you know where they've been taken?' she asked the old man.

'To Petrapole border. At least that's what I've been told.'

As soon as the words had left his mouth, Shefali wound the end of her sari tightly around her middle and started running towards the platform. The train for Bongaon had just started moving. She leapt into it and started looking around for a known face. But she couldn't find any. She got out at Bongaon station and asked a ticket checker, 'Where is Petrapole?' The man pointed out the direction with his forefinger. Shefali ran down the length of the platform towards Station Road and, covering the distance in a few minutes, came to Jessore Road. She went on and on, pushing past crowds gathered outside shops and houses, her feet not stopping for a minute. People stared at her. She looked like a demented creature, her clothes in disarray, her hair waving wildly about her back and shoulders.

'Where are you going, Didi?' a rickshaw puller asked curiously, as she raced across the bridge.

'Petrapole.'

'Get into my rickshaw, I'll take you…'

Shefali didn't bother to answer him. She didn't stop running either. When totally out of breath she would sit somewhere for a few minutes then start running again. Her feet slipped from time to time and she fell to the ground, grazing her knees and elbows. But these small accidents didn't make a dent in her resolution. She rose immediately afterwards and went on. The tears she couldn't control, despite all her efforts, fell in streams from her eyes down her cheeks to her breast.

The sun was sinking in the west by the time she reached her destination. In front of her was a flowering raintree with a brick structure under it. It had a tin roof from which a long pole rose with a flag fluttering atop. From the number of policemen with batons guarding it, she realized that this was the Border Office where her husband was being kept as a prisoner till the time he could be carried along with others of his kind, by boat across the river. Shefali started walking purposefully towards the building.

'*Ei!* Halt!' a man in a constable's uniform accosted her. 'Where are you going?'

Shefali pretended not to hear. She quickened her steps.

'*Ei! Ei!*' The constable ran after her. Shefali started running faster. But, after a few yards, she had to stop. An immense bamboo barricade stood in her way. And, now, more policemen and other officials came running in from different directions.

'Where are you going? What do you want?' A man in the uniform of a customs inspector walked towards her and asked in a threatening tone.

Shefali tried to speak but anxiety and exhaustion had robbed her of her voice. She stood still and took a few deep breaths. 'Petrapole,' she said at last.

'This is Petrapole border. What is your business here?'

'I'm looking for my husband.'

'Who's your husband?'

'You took him away at dead of night,' Shefali shouted, 'and you have the gall to ask me who he is.'

'How do you know we took your husband away?'

'The neighbours saw you. You dragged everyone from our slum while they lay sleeping, pushed them into lorries and are keeping them here as prisoners.'

And now another man, a senior police officer, emerged on the scene. 'What is the matter?' he asked curiously. Talking to Shefali at some length, he tried to assess the situation. 'You say your husband was in the lorry?' he muttered in a puzzled voice. 'But they were all Bangladeshi immigrants. They've been sent to Benapole.'

'Where's Benapole?'

'Right there. On the other bank.'

'I'm going…' Shefali started walking purposefully in the direction of the pointing finger.

'How will you go? Do you have a passport?' The officer stood in front of her, barring her way.

'What passport?' Shefali cried out angrily. 'I'm going to my husband. How dare you try to stop me?'

'That's not possible, Didi,' the man said quietly, reasonably. 'Your husband was an illegal immigrant from Bangladesh. We have sent him back from where he came. We've acted strictly on the orders of the government.'

'My husband is an illegal immigrant you say!' Suddenly a shriek tore out of Shefali's lungs, so loud that sky, land and river reverberated with the sound. 'What about me? What am I? I carry his child in my womb. Who will take care of us? We were two together, man and wife. We made a living, a hard one, but we never complained. We never troubled anybody. And now … what is to become of me and my child? *O go, Ma go! Ki hobe, Ma!'*

Bursting into tears Shefali dashed her head, over and over again, on the bamboo barricade.

Constable, customs inspector and police officer stood frozen in their places. They glanced at one another. No one had an answer.

The Witch

Tarashankar Bandyopadhyay

No one knows who gave the tract of land its name. Or when it was given. Those facts have been lost and buried in the annals of history. But the name has survived to this day as a vibrant reminder of its past glory. Chhaati Phataar Maath—the field of the bursting chest. There is no water here. Nor a speck of shade. No trees. Only a few thorny bushes of seyakul and khairi. The land stretches to the horizon in a shimmering sheet at the end of which the clumps of trees that signify the existence of villages appear as a dark blur. Looking on it the heart grows heavy, the mind listless. Travellers walking from one end to another are apt to lose their lives, their chests bursting from thirst, by the side of some ancient waterbody—dead and dry for centuries. The number of deaths increase in the summer months. In this season, it seems as though Chhaati Phataar Maath springs into a new unholy life. Its tongue slavers for the taste of blood and it exercises all its powers to attain the dimensions of a mighty pestilence. Dust, dense as smoke, rises in swirls from the ground, higher and higher, till it meets the sky. Burning heat and the stench of death hit the unwary traveller's senses. But he sees nothing, for the thick pall hanging in the air renders Chhaati Phataar Maath invisible to the human eye.

Tiny hamlets dot the four sides of this field. They have simple homesteads in which unlettered peasants live. They tell a story, heard over generations, of a gigantic snake that once lived in Chhaati Phataar Maath. The poisonous fumes from its nostrils gradually destroyed all animate and inanimate life. Trees and animals perished. Even the birds and insects flying in the air felt their wings singe and crumble to ash and dropped to the ground like dead leaves straight into the jaws of the mighty reptile.

That snake is no more, but some of its power still clings to the atmosphere. Chhaati Phataar Maath is cursed territory. To its east is a marshy tract which the locals call Daldalir Jalaa. Daldalir Jalaa had been a shallow bog of slime and rotting vegetation, the size of a lake, till the Sahas of Ramnagar bought the land, drained it and planted mango saplings. In time, these grew into fine trees. But alas! Forty years ago, an old witch with fearful powers of destruction took possession of the orchard and made her home there.

People are still afraid of going near her, for her ruthlessness is well-known. Children see her at a distance and run for safety. Yet everyone can describe her. Her matted hair, crooked limbs and, best of all, her eyes. Those eyes, they say, have not blinked in forty years. Beneath one of the mango trees is an earthen hovel. It has only one room with a dawa, a veranda thatched with straw, jutting out of it. The witch sits here all day long, her body still as a statue. Her unwavering gaze is fixed on Chhaati Phataar Maath.

She gets up once a day to sweep the earthen floors and smear them with cow dung. That done, she goes to the village to beg. She doesn't need to stand outside many doors. Two or three are sufficient, for the housewives are afraid of her and pour more rice into her tattered anchal than they need to, in the belief that their generosity would keep her evil eye away from their husbands and children. Once she is able to collect a seer of rice, she stops begging for the day.

On the way back she stops at the grocer's and exchanges half her stock for some salt, mustard oil, chillies and kerosene. She goes out once more in search of kindling. She picks up whatever she can find. Fallen leaves and twigs, dried cowpats and bits of broken bamboo. Once she has cooked and eaten her meal there is nothing left for her to do except sit on her perch and stare unblinkingly on Chhaati Phataar Maath.

The old woman does not belong to these parts. No one knows where she was born. But of one thing everyone is certain. She had lived in three or four villages in the vicinity and destroyed them all. Then, forty years ago, she had darted across the skies on a flying tree and looked down on Chhaati Phataar Maath. Charmed by its desolate splendour, she had come down and made her home there. Beings like her prefer to live in isolation. Human society frightens them. For, the moment they see a human being, a deep-rooted instinct to hurt and destroy flares into life. This malignant force hisses like the tongue of a snake and spews venom into the air. Fanning out like the hood of a cobra, the unholy urge dances in glee. Powerless to control this, she submits to its strength. After all she, too, is human. The knowledge of her own power makes her shiver. She has a mirror, dim and dusty with age, in which she examines her face from time to time. Two eyes look back at her, tiny eyes with bronze irises, the lights from them sharp and glittering as knives. Her hair is the colour of shredded jute, her mouth a gaping hole. Looking at her reflection she feels a stab of fear. Her lips tremble and turn blue. She puts the mirror down and looks out again on Chhaati Phataar Maath.

The wooden frame of the mirror has blackened with age. It had been a lovely rose brown, gleaming with polish. The glass, now spotted with mildew, once had the shining clarity of a sun-warmed lake. The face that had looked out of it had been another face. A small forehead surrounded by waves of hair. Not black; dark brown with reddish glints. Below the arched eyebrows a delicate nose rose in an aquiline curve. The eyes were small even then, but they shone like pieces of topaz. People were afraid of her eyes, but she loved them. Crinkling them even smaller she felt as though she could see the full expanse of sky from one end to another. Those razor-slit eyes had a strange power. Whomever they looked upon with love came to harm. She had no idea of how it happened. But it did.

She remembers the first day…

*

She was standing on a cracked slab of the ancient bank of Durga Sagar Lake facing the shrine of Burho Shibtala. She could see herself in the water, undulating, changing contours. Her body was swaying, growing longer and longer. All at once the ripples ceased and she saw herself whole and clear. A pretty ten-year-old girl looking at her with a shy smile. Suddenly she felt a tug at her head. Haru Sarkar, of the Brahmin palli, was behind her. Seizing the hair at her nape he twisted it viciously. '*Haramjadi!*' he roared, throwing her down on the broken flags. 'How dare you cast an evil eye on my son? I'll kill you.'

She remembers the hate and revulsion on Haru Sarkar's face to this day…

'*O go*, Babu!' she had cried out in terror. 'I don't know what I have done! I beg you…'

'I'll tell you what you have done. The boy has been tossing and turning, screaming with belly cramps ever since you left the house. If your tongue had watered with greed when you saw him eating his *muri* with milk and mangoes why didn't you ask for some, you bitch?'

It was true. The saliva had gushed into her mouth at the sight. But why that should give the boy a bellyache she hadn't a clue. She wonders about it to this day. She remembers going to Haru Babu's house and falling at his wife's feet. Crying and praying, *Make him well, O Thakur! Make the boy well. Here ... I take back the evil glance I cast on him.*

Then the strangest thing happened. The boy vomited a couple of times and rose from the bed, completely cured. A relieved Haru Sarkar turned to his wife. 'Give her some muri and a mango,' he said. Sarkar ginni picked up a broom and waved it in the girl's face. 'Muri and mango indeed!' she hissed. 'I'll stuff her greedy mouth with ashes hot from the *chulo!* I've taken pity on her and given her food whenever she came to the house. *A poor orphan girl* ... I've thought. And the ungrateful witch returns my goodness by casting her evil eye on my son! Look, look at those eyes. I've had my suspicions for a long time. I've taken care never to feed the children in her presence. She snuck in today when I was away at the ghat and did this vile thing.'

Trembling with shame and fear the girl had run away. The story had spread in the village and people had started shunning her. Not allowed in any house, she had slept that night on the portico of the shrine of Burho Shibtala. No ... she hadn't slept. She had kept awake all night weeping bitterly, praying, *O go, Thakur! Purge my eyes of the unholy power. If not, strike me blind.*

*

The old woman stirs. A deep sigh escapes her. The thin lips quiver; tears glitter in the tiny eyes. She knows, now, why God was unable to answer her prayer. The malignant power she bore was her punishment for the sins of a past life. She had to live with it. What could poor God do? It was wrong to blame him…

That night she had decided never to cross a householder's threshold again. She would stand outside the door and beg the way other beggars did. It had been difficult the first time. Her throat was choked, and her tongue refused to articulate the words. But she forced herself and suddenly they came out in high unnatural tones. '*Ma go!* Can I be given some alms, Ma? *Hari bol! Hari bol!*'

'*Ke re?* Who is that? Oh, it's you. Stand where you are. Don't dare come into the house.'

'No, Ma. I won't come in.'

But the very next moment a strange feeling had come over her. A greedy craving rose from her belly like a darting flame and made the saliva squirt into her mouth. What a lovely smell was coming from the kitchen! They were frying fish. Big fat chunks of fresh fish. She sucked in her cheeks. *A ha ha!* She breathed deeply.

'*Ei … ei haramjadi!* Look … look at her peeping into the kitchen with her snake eyes!'

Chhi! Chhi! Chhi! The memory makes her bite her tongue in shame. She had peeped into the kitchen and her eyes had searched it from one end to another. It was not the first time that such a despicable urge had risen in her. Nor the last. It does … to this day.

The motionless form, once moulded out of rich earth, is dilapidated now; the colour of dust. Slowly, the chipped joints of the ancient limbs flex and loosen. Breaking out of their shackles they shudder into life. The twisted nails dig into the earth of the dawa. The white head bobs up and down in agitation. *Why do these things happen?* She has asked herself the question over and over again, all her life, but never found the answer. What should she do about it? What *could* she do? If only somebody would tell her. *Aanh! Aanh! Aanh!* She squeals in the voice of a beaten beast. Clamping her toothless gums in helpless rage she raises her hands to her dreadlocks and pulls them cruelly by the roots. Her eyes, sharp as a kite's, scan the endless sweep of empty earth.

It is the month of Chaitra, the last month of the year and the first of the hot season. The cool of the morning has given way to a blazing afternoon. A haze of heat and dust shimmers over Chhaati Phataar Maath rendering it almost invisible. But the razor-sharp eyes can see better than most. What was that trail of light flickering across the field? She could, if she wished, have blown the dust away with a puff from her lips and seen what it was. Ah ... it was gone now, but she could see something else. Something solid, substantial, in the smoky haze. *Arre!* It was moving. What was it? A living being? Human? Yes, yes, she could see it now. It was a woman.

Suddenly the old hateful urge rose from within her. Should she blow a breath on the creature and make it disappear? Her toothless mouth opened in a cackle of cruel laughter. She rocked herself to and fro like a mad woman.

And then she pulled herself together. Balling her fists till the sharp nails dug into her flesh she fought the bloodthirsty urge. No ... no ... she would turn her eyes away. She wouldn't look towards Chhaati Phataar Maath. If she did, the poor woman would die of asphyxiation. She would sweep the floor of her hut instead. Or she could stack the dry leaves and twigs she had gathered that morning into neat piles...

Unlocking her inert limbs, she picks up the broom and starts sweeping the floor. But the dust and leaves she gathers together take on a life of their own. Wriggling away from the end of her broom, they coil around her form like snakes, hissing and spitting at the withered skin. Dust stings her eyes and nostrils. She doesn't know how to withstand the assault. She bares her empty gums like a mangy old cat. 'Out!' she shrieks, waving her broom helplessly in the air. 'Out I say! Leave me alone.' But the snakes do not heed her. They wind about her form tighter and tighter till she can scarcely breathe. 'Out! Out!' she howls in despair, flailing herself with the broom. Suddenly, with cackles of rasping laughter, the snakes release her from their coils. Loosening their hold, they fly, as though on wings, in the direction of Chhaati Phataar Maath. Dust and dead khairi rise in swirls to greet them and together they form a giant tower that spirals its way to the sky. More such columns spring up in the air. Spinning in a joyous dance. There are a thousand now. Big and small. Chhaati Phataar Maath grows dark and terrifying.

Looking at the scene, the old crone is filled with glee. Waves of rapture lap her form. She chortles with laughter. Raising her bent body, she spreads out her arms, broom in one hand. She twirls her limbs, slowly at first, then fast … faster. Round and round she goes, round and round, till overcome by fatigue, she sinks to the ground. She tries to stand up and resume her dance, but her legs will not support her. Her head spins and the world grows dark. Her chest crackles with thirst. Dropping on her hands and feet she crawls, like a baby, to the clay pot of water in the corner of her room…

*

'Is anyone at home? *O go!* Is anyone at home? Can I come in?'

'*Ke?* Who is that?'

A young woman, coated with dust from head to foot, poked a long pale face through the door. She was clutching something to her breast, hiding it under her tattered anchal. It was dark within and all she could see was a knot of crooked limbs huddled together like a bunch of rotten twigs. She felt a stab of fear and moved back a few steps.

'Water,' she murmured faintly, 'a drop of water.'

The old woman sat up slowly.

'*A ha ha*! My poor child,' she clicked her tongue in sympathy. 'Come in. Sit down and rest yourself.'

The girl's frightened eyes darted this way and that. Then, slowly, reluctantly, she seated herself at the farthest edge of the dawa.

'Give me a drink of water, Ma,' she said faintly. 'I am dying of thirst.'

The old woman's heart melted. She poured out a large tumbler of water, then, digging a bony hand into another pot, she groped for a piece of gur, murmuring all the while, 'Poor child! Poor child! What made you think of crossing that field of death in this terrible heat? You could have died.'

'I'm on my way to see my sick mother. Her village lies at the eastern boundary. But I lost my way and found myself in the middle of Chhaati Phataar Maath.'

Hobbling towards the dawa with the water and gur, the old woman got a shock. A male infant, a few months old, was lying on the floor. The poor mite was drenched in sweat and his tiny limbs sagged like boiled spinach.

'Come, come,' she prompted, pushing the tumbler towards the girl. 'Sprinkle some on the child's face. Quick!'

The girl obeyed. Wetting her anchal with water, she wiped the tiny face and limbs and poured some into his mouth.

The old crone sat and watched them from a distance. The woman was young and healthy and the infant, perhaps her first, had a plump tender body, moist and supple as a tendril on a bottle gourd vine. Saliva squirted into her toothless mouth. She sucked in her cheeks and swallowed.

A ha re! The child's chest was going up and down like a pair of bellows. Perspiration was pouring out of him. More and more and more. A patch of damp was forming on the earthen floor on which he lay. The eyes were misting, turning crimson. Was it … was it? What would she do? What *could* she do? Why did they come into her presence? Why? The strangest sensations were pricking in her blood. A frantic urge to pick up the bundle of human flesh and hold it to her breast. To squeeze and mash it, like a pat of dough, against her ribbed, hollowed chest. To press the cool, watery limbs against her fevered skin.

Baap re! How the child was sweating! All the water was being drained out of his body. She knew it from the sap that was filling her own mouth … warm and sweet. Oozing from the corners. Dribbling down her chin.

'*O re kheye phellam re!*' An anguished cry tore its way from her throat. 'I'm … I'm swallowing the child. Run. Run for your life. Pick up your baby and run!'

The young woman who was drinking water in large thirsty gulps looked up with a gasp. The tumbler clattered to the ground.

'You!' she whispered, her face as white as a sheet. 'Is this Ramnagar? Are you … the one?'

Without waiting for an answer, she snatched up the child and flew out of the house, the little one hanging from her arms like a fledgling folded in a mother bird's wings. The old woman watched her flight. The tiny eyes dimmed with self-pity. She was helpless. If it were possible, she would have pierced her sharp twirling nails into her withered breast and torn the shameless urge out of it. She would have cut off her tongue. But all this, she knew, was useless. The malaise lay deeper. Far deeper.

Chhi! Chhi! Chhi! How would she set foot on the village path tomorrow? How would she show her face? The child would be dead by then and everyone would know the reason. They wouldn't taunt her with it. They wouldn't dare. But the disgust and hate in their eyes would shame her more than words. Even now children ran away at the sight of her. They burst out weeping. Some even fainted and fell to the ground. *Chhi! Chhi! Chhi!*

A similar self-aversion had led her to flee the village of her birth, in the dark of night, years ago. She was a little less older then—approaching womanhood. A friend of hers, a girl from her own community, had delivered a male child the night before and she had gone to see him. Savitri was sitting in the yard sunning her limbs, her new-born lying beside her on a kantha. What a lovely baby! Plump and healthy with a shining dark skin. She felt her heart swell with love. She wanted to fondle the tiny bundle and squeeze it against her breast. To kiss the drooling mouth with hungry lips. She was unaware, then, of the evil power in her. She thought her feelings were those of maternal love.

All of a sudden, Savitri's mother-in-law came rushing in. '*Haramjadi!*' she screamed at her daughter-in-law. 'Have you lost your mind? Chattering and giggling with the accursed creature! If anything happens to my grandson, I'll flay you alive.' Then, turning to the visitor, she pointed to the door and said grimly, 'Get out, you slit-eyed witch. Don't dare come here again.'

Savitri's limbs, still weak from childbirth, had trembled in fear. Picking up the baby she had run indoors and slammed the door. And *she*? She had walked out of the house, head hung in humiliation. Tears had gathered in her eyes. Everyone said she was a witch. They could be right. She did not know. But even if she was a witch, would she, ever, ever harm Savitri's baby? *Dear God*, she prayed, *be the judge and prove them all wrong. Give the boy one hundred years. Let everyone know how much I love Savitri's child.*

As afternoon came on, the mother-in-law's fears began manifesting themselves as the indelible truth. News rippled through the village and reached her ears. The baby was very sick. The tiny limbs were flailing and threshing, and the small trunk was twisting into an arch. Turning blue. Exactly as though some malignant creature was sucking the lifeblood out of him.

She had run away in shame. Avoiding the village paths, she had pushed her way through the jungle and taken refuge in the burning ghat. She had hidden herself behind a bamboo thicket and thought of what she had done. But … but if she had drunk blood, as everyone was saying, it would be in her mouth, would it not? Crouching on her haunches she spat on the ground. *Thoo! Thoo!* Several times. But where was the blood? Her spit was as innocently white as foaming milk. She dug her fingers into her throat and threw up. Yes, now she could see some dark flecks in her vomit. She dug deeper and a gush of fresh blood filled her mouth, warm and salty.

There was no doubt in her mind now. What people said was right. She possessed a demoniac power which surfaced whenever she looked on any human being with love in her heart. Love turned sour in her; took the form of hate and destruction…

⋆

It was well past midnight. Was it the fourteenth day of the waxing moon? Yes, of course it was. The old woman could hear the beating of the drums from the temple of Tara Devi. Tomorrow it will be purnima, the night of the full moon. The shrine would be full of people. They would sacrifice goats and ask for boons. Tara Ma was a powerful deity and no one who approached her for favours went away disappointed. Only *she* had been denied Tara Ma's blessing. She had offered prayers year after year and begged, 'Take pity on me, Ma. Change me from a witch to an ordinary woman. I'll slit my breast and offer my blood.' But the Goddess hadn't heeded her prayers. A deep sigh rose from the shrivelled chest. Sorrow and despair were her constant companions now. She didn't even resent them anymore. Thoughts drifted through her head like kites on broken strings. Floating this way and that on the whims of the wind. Dipping to the ground. A lost look came into the aged yellow eyes. She sat motionless looking on Chhaati Phataar Maath. There was nothing to see. Only a dun-coloured pall of dust. Still and unwavering. Not a whiff of breeze to stir it…

*

The child died a few hours later. While the woman was still on her way to her mother's house. Nothing she did would stop the perspiration that kept pouring out of him. Perspiration? Or was it something else? Someone was drawing the life blood out of him, sucking him dry. And who could it be but the diabolic creature in whose hut she had taken shelter? Whose water she had poured down the baby's throat?

'*O go!* What have I done?' She beat her breast and howled, 'What possessed me to go there? To let the wicked creature set her eyes on my little darling? *O go! Ma go!*' The villagers gathered around the weeping woman and her dead child. Some commiserated with her. Some cursed and threatened the witch.

A band of ruffians made their way to her hut, vowing revenge. She saw them from afar and started muttering in self-defence, 'It wasn't my fault. Why did she come to my house? Why did she hold out the beautiful baby before my eyes?' Suddenly she felt a current of mixed emotions sweep through her. A shiver ran down her spine and the hair on her head stood up and spread around her face like a cobra's hood. She screamed abuses at the approaching men in a voice that was no longer human. It was a predator bird's screech, shrill and penetrating.

Her would-be assaulters turned pale with fear and backed away. But the old woman's fury had not abated. Curses, bitter and corrosive, continued to fall from her lips, spiked with the poison she had held in her breast for so many years. Her breath came out, hot and hissing, like a wounded snake's. Her arms, the skin on them thin and papery as a bat's wing, flailed the earth. And then she started laughing. An ear-splitting metallic laugh burst from her, ringing through the length and breadth of Chhaati Phataar Maath. She pulled her hair by the roots, weeping and laughing by turns.

Tck! Tck! Tck! she cackled like a brooding hen. 'What fun! No need to light the kitchen fire. No need to set rice on the boil. I've devoured a whole human child. Sucked it dry. I've had my fill for the day.'

Night came on. It was the ninth night of *shukla paksha* and Chhaati Phataar Maath lay shrouded in silvery moonlight. *Jhir... jhir... jhir...* a gentle breeze rippled the leaves of the mango trees. Crickets chirped and an unknown bird's song, sweet and fluty, came wafting on the air. The old woman pricked up her ears. She could hear voices from behind her hut. Had the goons of the morning returned to harm her? She rose and turned the corner on cautious feet. There was a couple standing under the gopal bhog tree at the edge of the stream. She knew them. The Bauri girl whose husband had abandoned her and the boy she loved. She crouched on the ground, a few yards away, listening.

'I'm going home,' the girl whispered. 'Someone may see us.'

Heh! Heh! Her companion laughed away her fears. 'No one comes here even during the day. As if they'll come at night.'

'Even so,' the girl persisted. 'I'm not staying here with you. Your father isn't allowing us to marry. Then what's the point...?'

Chhi! Chhi! Chhi! The old woman bit her tongue. If the two were in love and wanted a quiet place to meet, why didn't they come into her hut? Why stand outside where someone might see them? Were they embarrassed to take her help? But why? She was an old woman; their grandmother's age. She understood their situation and predicament...

And now the boy was saying something that made the withered lips curl with amusement. 'If we are not allowed to marry,' he whispered, 'we'll run away and settle in another village as far from here as possible. I cannot live without you.'

Aah maran! The old woman snorted in contempt. *Can't live without her indeed! A girl as black and round bellied as a clay pot!*

Suddenly another scene came before her eyes. Another time. Another place. She had seen someone in the long mirror that hung over a wall of the paan shop in Bolpur. A tall slim girl, about fourteen or fifteen years old, with a head of rough reddish hair, a small forehead, a delicate nose and thin lips. The eyes were small, it was true, but attractive ... bright brown with golden flecks. Charmed with her own beauty she had kept smiling at her image. She had never seen herself in a mirror before.

'*Arre!* Who in the world are you?' A man's voice came to her ears. She looked up. A young man, tall and strapping, stood before her, 'Where do you come from?'

This had happened on the day after the incident in Savitri's house. She had run away from the village that same night and come to Bolpur. She had liked the look of the man but taken umbrage at his tone.

'Where I come from is my business.' She had glared at him. 'Not yours.'

'Your business! Not mine! Do you know who you are talking to? One blow and you'll fall to the ground like a dead leaf. Have you seen the size of my fist?'

She had stared at the stranger. At the sculptured black marble torso, the strong thighs rippling with muscles, and had willed herself to suck the blood out of him. She had gritted her teeth and mouthed a stream of silent curses. Her tongue had watered like a fountain. But nothing happened. Throwing a bitter glance at him she left the place.

She encountered him again the same day. She was sitting on a bank of the big pond at the far end of Bolpur town, beyond the railway line, eating *muri* from a heap in her anchal. The sun had just set, and a saffron moon was rising like an enormous platter from the east. The light hadn't turned silver yet. The sky was covered in a dim yellow haze. Suddenly she heard footsteps approach and looked up in alarm. It was the man of the morning.

'Why did you run away?' he asked, laughing. 'I only asked you a question.'

She remembers the laugh to this day and the two dimples that pitted his cheeks...

'I don't want to answer your question. Please go away. I'll scream if you don't.'

'You'll scream, will you? I'll wring your little neck before a squeak comes out and bury you in the weeds and slime.' He pointed to the pond. 'No one will find you again. Ever.'

She had looked at him with terror-stricken eyes and remained silent. All of a sudden, he stamped his foot and shouted '*Dhat!*' Jumping up in fright at his menacing tone she burst into tears. The muri fell out of her lap and rolled all over the bank. The man was embarrassed.

'You little ninny,' he said in a softened voice. 'Stop snivelling.'

He smiled as he spoke and there was tenderness in his voice. But that hadn't taken away her fear.

'You're not going to beat me, are you?' she had asked between sobs.

'*Arre na.* Why should I beat you? All I did was ask you where you've come from and you snapped my head off. That's why…'

He started laughing once more, the dimples deepening in his cheeks.

'I've come from far. V-e-r-y far. All the way from Patharghata.'

'What's your name? What caste are you?'

'My name is Shordhoni. Everyone calls me Shora. We're doms.

'I'm a dom too.' The man sounded pleased. 'So … tell me. What made you run away from home?'

The tears brimmed into her eyes again. She remained silent, not knowing what to say.

'Did you have a fight with your parents?'

'I have no parents.'

'Then…?'

'There's no one to look after me in the village. No one to give me food and shelter. I came to the town to work for a living.'

'Why didn't you get married?'

Married! She had looked at the stranger with wonder in her eyes. What was he saying? Who would marry a witch like her? But … there was something in his voice that was unnerving her. She trembled and a strange shyness came over her. She felt her cheeks flush and her heart beat with an unknown emotion. She lowered her eyes and her fingers fiddled with the broken stones of the bank…

Suddenly the needle with which she was stitching her old memories fell to the ground. The thread snapped and her mind went blank. But the shy rapture of that moment stayed with her. The old woman sat with her head bowed like a young girl in the first flush of love. As on that evening, her hands moved involuntarily, gathering leaves and pebbles into a mound.

Oof! There was a cloud of mosquitoes swarming around her. Humming like bees from a broken hive. Why! The pair under the gopal bhog tree must have left. She couldn't hear their voices anymore. She rose softly and crept back to her perch smiling to herself. They would be back tomorrow. There was no other place in the village more suitable for a lovers' meeting. No one dared come near her hut. But those two would come. Love knew no fear.

And now a strange feeling came upon her. The old urge was rising; the urge to hurt and annihilate. Should she suck the blood from the young man's body? Such a strong, supple, muscular body! But the very next moment she shook her head violently. No … no … never. She mouthed the words. He was young and in love. No harm should come to him. She sat silent for a few minutes then started swaying gently, thoughts running in and out of her head. She was carrying a burden already. As heavy as a block of iron. She had drunk the blood of an innocent child. There would be no sleep for her tonight.

She wished she could cross Chhaati Phataar Maath and go far away … very far away. People said she had special powers. She could put wings on a tree and make it take her wherever she wished. How wonderful it would be if that were true! If she could sit peacefully in a cluster of leaves and be borne over the sky, drifting on cool breezes, floating between clouds. But then … then she wouldn't see the young couple again. They would be sure to come tomorrow…

*

Hee! Hee! Hee! The lad was here. She could see him sitting by the stream, his eyes darting this way and that. He was waiting for his beloved. Her eyes twinkled with amused affection. *Be patient*, the withered lips murmured reassurance, *she'll come*. A scene such as this had played itself out in her own life years and years ago. It came before her eyes, sharp and clear. The young man who had accosted her near the pond had returned the next day. To the same place; at the same time. He was sitting on the bank swinging his legs and gazing on the path which she would take.

'You've come! I've been waiting for ages.'

The old woman was startled. It was the boy's voice. He was speaking to the girl who had walked in silently through the trees. But what a coincidence! The young dom who had waited for her had spoken exactly the same words. She had pursed her lips and looked demure. She couldn't see very well in the dark, but she could swear that the girl had the same expression on her face. The young man had brought a leaf cone full of kochuri and gaja that day. 'Eat,' he had said, holding it out to her. 'You dropped your muri yesterday because of me.'

But she hadn't put out her hand. She couldn't. The strangest emotions were coming over her. Desire, swift and sudden, was leaping up in her blood. Swaying and swinging like a snake to a snake charmer's flute. Venom and fangs forgotten, it was tossing its head in an ecstatic dance. And then? What had he done then? The memory made her blush. The youngsters of today, she thought smiling, have no idea ... *O Ma! O Ma!* The boy was doing exactly the same thing! He was putting something, was it a gaja, in the girl's mouth. Filled with glee, the old crone flailed her arms in the air and laughed quietly to herself.

Suddenly she stopped laughing. Stifling a sigh, she leaned against a tree trunk lost in thought. The strangest thing had happened next. The young man had looked at her with unblinking eyes and asked, 'Will you marry me, Shora?'

She was so startled she lost her voice. She could feel her ears blazing and her hands and feet grow cold and clammy. Sweat rolled off her forehead in large drops.

'I work in Marwari Babu's factory. I earn lots of money. But no one in Bolpur is ready to give his daughter to me. That's because I am an untouchable. But you and I are from the same caste and we're both orphans.' He had held her light eyes with his fine dark ones. 'Marry me, Shora,' he had urged...

The two sitting by the stream were speaking softly but the silence around them was so deep she could hear every word. 'The people of the village are against us,' the boy was saying, 'your family as well as mine. They're making life hell for us. Let's run away. We'll go to some distant village where nobody knows us. We'll marry and be happy.'

O Ma! O Ma! That was exactly what she and the young dom had done. They had cut off ties with everyone in the world and built themselves a shack by the side of the factory. His work was stoking the fire under an enormous barrel-like contraption called a *boila* or something like it. He was paid higher wages than all the other workers.

'N-o-o-o.' The girl's voice came to her ears, sulky, demanding. 'You'll have to buy me silver bangles first. And tie a ten-rupee note in my anchal. Only then I'll go with you. I'm not ready to starve in a faraway village for want of money.'

Chhi! Chhi! Chhi! The old woman spat on the ground in disgust. She felt like thrashing the girl with her broomstick. Did she have no faith in her man? Such a strong, sturdy handsome youth who loved her so much! Would such a man let her starve? 'Death to you,' she muttered indignantly. 'Silver bangles indeed! Why … if you stay loyal to him, you'll wear conch bangles encased in gold one day. *Chhi!*'

The girl waited for a reply but there was none.

'Why don't you speak?' she snapped at him. 'Have you gone dumb? Say what you have to say quickly. I can't wait here all night.'

The boy sighed. A deep sigh that hung on the air for a long time. 'What is there to say?' he murmured. 'If I had the money, I would give it to you. And the bangles too. I wouldn't have waited for you to ask.'

'I'm going.' The girl tossed her head and walked away, swaying her hips lasciviously.

'Go.'

'Don't call me anymore.'

'Very well.'

She left. Her white sari melted into the moonlight and disappeared. The dejected lover kept sitting by the stream, his head in his hands. Poor lad! The old crone clicked her tongue sadly. What would he do now? Would he leave the village never to return? Or would he, God forbid, take his own life? Drown in the pond or hang himself? No … no. He mustn't do that. It would be better for him to give the girl the silver bangles. She had twenty-one rupees hidden in a clay pot in her hut. She could give him two out of it. Or even five. Five rupees would be enough. Once she got her bangles the girl wouldn't make any more fuss. *Aa ha!* He was so young! Youth was the time for love. For happiness. She would give the boy five rupees and tell him to look on her as his grandmother. She would laugh and joke with him. She would wipe the sorrow from his face.

She rose slowly, painfully, putting her weight on her hands. She tried to straighten the hump on her back but it was as stiff and heavy as stone. Hobbling towards the stream she called out with a merry laugh, 'Poor little downcast lover! Do not despair. Your troubles are about to end. I'll give you…'

The boy looked up startled. He saw a strange creature creeping towards him in the dark, closer and closer, like a giant crab. And now a face was thrust into his. A face as ridged and contorted as a dried mango. And out of the ridges two tiny eyes glowed like pinpoints of amber light. The mouth was a gaping cavern. The boy's blood froze. His heart started hammering like a blacksmith's anvil. Springing up, he ran screaming into the woods.

Within seconds the old woman's face changed. The amused indulgence vanished and hate and loathing took its place. The hackles on her neck rose like an angry cat's and her narrow eyes glittered with venom. Pulling her lips back from her toothless gums she snarled at the fleeing figure. 'Die!' she screeched. 'Die!' And now the old urge rose, snaking up from deep within her bowels. She would destroy the ungrateful creature; suck all the blood out of him. Not only the blood. Flesh, fat, sinews, bones and marrow … she felt like consuming them all.

Suddenly the boy sank to the ground with a howl of agony. Then, picking himself up, he limped his way slowly through the trees. She could see him no longer.

Next morning a rumour spread through the village, leaving everyone turned to stone. The she-devil who lived by the stream had shot a Bauri boy with a flying missile. He had gone there in the evening and the bloodsucking fiend had smelled his presence the way a tigress smells her prey. She had crawled stealthily towards him, not making a sound. Then, when the frightened boy had tried to escape, she had brought him sprawling to the ground by blowing a dart through her lips. It was sticking to his heel when he reached home, a long thin bone sharp as a needle. The boy had tried to pull it out but it was stuck so deep, the blood had gurgled out like a fountain. High fever and convulsions had wracked him through the night and now his body was arching as though some malignant spirit had seized him by the head and feet and was squeezing the blood out of him.

The news reached the old woman's ears. She tried to feel concern but couldn't. An inexplicable apathy came over her. Never in her life had she felt so weary, so listless. The boy was dying. But what could she do about it? He shouldn't have tried to run away. How dare the little weakling run away from her? Even the toughest, most stout-hearted man she had known in her life, a man who had warred with fire all his waking hours, had not escaped her evil power.

More news came the next day. The boy's father had sent for a clairvoyant who had promised to cure him. The old woman shrugged. The physician in Bolpur had said the same thing. He would cure her husband. But was a slow fever with a dry wracking cough a disease? He had left medicines, but they hadn't helped. The symptoms had persisted. And, little by little, the flesh had fallen from the magnificent limbs and the skin that had once gleamed like polished ebony had turned to ash. What had happened to him? And why did he vomit blood in the end?

Her eyes looked out on Chhaati Phataar Maath. It lay like a bleached corpse under the midday sun. Not a breath of wind anywhere. Not a leaf stirred. A strange restlessness seized her. She rose from her perch and walked about in the yard. Round and round she went, her thoughts running ahead of her. She had loved the man more than life itself. She had given him all she had to give. Heart, soul, mind and body. Yet she couldn't protect him from her own evil power. It had drained him of his life force. Emaciated his body and left it dry and brittle as a fish bone.

Suddenly she laughed. A harsh metallic laugh that rang through the length and breadth of Chhaati Phataar Maath. Who was this clairvoyant who thought he could cure the Bauri boy? She had cast a malevolent glance on the fleeing figure, hadn't she? There was no way he could counter that. Not all the clairvoyants in the world could save him.

Oof! How hot and still the air was. She could barely breathe. She felt a weight on her chest. Suffocating her; crushing her lungs. Was the clairvoyant using his powers on her? Mouthing his most deadly mantra? Perhaps he was. It didn't matter. Let him do the best he can, she thought scornfully. But the pain … the pain was excruciating. It was killing her. If only her heart would burst open, and the grief and agony she had held in it for decades well out in blessed release.

One thing was certain. She couldn't live here anymore. She would have to escape the irate villagers. They would come after her any moment now, as the people of Bolpur had done after her husband's death. They had hounded her out of the town. And all because of an indiscreet remark she had made to the wife of a worker in Marwari Babu's factory.

Shankari and her husband belonged to the Harhi community. Being fellow untouchables, a friendship had sprung up between the two women and they often confided in one another. Some days after her husband's death, out of a desperate need to lighten the load of guilt she carried, Shora had opened her heart to her friend. She had told her about the evil power she possessed; a power that destroyed everyone she loved.

What happened next? Well ... here she was living at the edge of a desolate tract of land at a safe distance from human habitation. She had fled from village to village, in the intervening years, but nowhere had she found a permanent home. It was time for her to move once more. But where would she go?

O Ki! The sound of lamentations, loud and bitter, tore the silence of the hot, somnolent afternoon. The old woman's blood froze with terror. She sat, immobile, for a while. Then, tossing her head this way and that like one possessed, she crawled into her room and locked the door. A few hours later she stepped out of her hut, a small bundle at her hip, and walked across Chhaati Phataar Maath... her slight form silhouetted against a twilit sky.

All of a sudden, the world went dark. A deep, dense, unnatural dark. A thin trail of dust followed the feet of the fleeing witch. All else was still. Chhaati Phataar Maath lay trapped and lifeless under a black velvet shroud.

After walking for a while, she sank to the ground. She couldn't take another step. Her heart was pounding with exhaustion and her hands and feet felt numb and heavy. *What do I do now?* she thought fearfully.

Suddenly, after years and years of frozen silence, a wail rose from her breast. A wail of lamentation for her dead husband.

'*O go!*' she cried out wildly. 'Come back. Come back to me.'

What was that? She looked up. The black cover had shifted, and she could see a part of the sky. It was the colour of her eyes. Moments later the storm broke. The first Kalbaisakhi of the season. Great clouds of dust rose from the earth and went spiralling across the field carried by cyclonic winds. Trees were pulled out by the roots. Animals were swept away. And the old woman…

*

Next morning, after the storm had subsided, the villagers found her hanging from a khairi bush at the extreme edge of Chhaati Phataar Maath. Her body, light and fluttering like a moth's, was pinned to the highest branch. There were patches of blood on the ground—the dark, unholy blood from a witch's veins. The men looked at one another. What had happened was obvious. She had tried to escape on her flying tree when a powerful mantra from the clairvoyant's lips had entered her breast and brought her tumbling down like a bird shot in the wing. She had fallen on the khairi bush and, pierced by hundreds of thorns, had died an agonizing death.

Today Chhaati Phataar Maath is deadlier than ever before. Mixed with the venom of a prehistoric snake is the blood of a malignant witch. Reeling under a pall of dust that clings to it from dawn till dusk, it stretches to unseen horizons…

And now some specks appear through the haze. Tiny black moving dots. They grow larger. Then sounds are heard. A mighty flapping of wings. A cloud of vultures is swooping down on Chhaati Phataar Maath.

Raikamal

Tarashankar Bandyopadhyay

A small akhara surrounded by a wattle fence. Through the gaps one can see a stretch of verdant green dotted with mango and guava trees, towering neems and bamboo clumps. In the centre of this charming garden is a little cottage with a couple of rooms and a yard swabbed smooth and clean with red earth. At one end of the yard a madhabi and a malati have formed a natural bower. Locked in an embrace they have flung leaves, stems and tendrils over a bamboo machaan. And, taking turns, they cover it with flowers throughout the year. The akhara is named Kamal Kunja.

Two women live here. Kamini, the Vaishnavi, follows her caste profession of gathering alms by clinking her cymbals outside the doors of the villagers and singing of the love of Radha and Krishna. And her daughter Kamalini, whose face is like the lotus after which she is named, swabs the yard, waters the garden and takes singing lessons from the elderly Baul, Rasik Das. His akhara, Rasa Kunja, is a short distance away but he spends most of his time here.

Rasik is the tallest man that ever lived. His neck is like a stork's, and his arms and legs so long and loose, they jerk with every movement. His hair is tied in a knot on the top of his head and his beard carefully plaited into a braid. Kamalini can't resist giggling whenever she sees him. '*Stork Babaji! Stork Babaji!*' she teases. Kamini is mortified at her daughter's lack of manners. '*Mar Mukhpuri*!' she curses. 'Huge hulking girl of fourteen! Do you have no sense?'

'*Na go na.*' Rasik smiles, 'Don't scold her. Her spirit is infused with the joy that was Radharani's. She is no ordinary Kamal. She's Raikamal.'

'Kamli!' Ranjan calls from beyond the fence. Kamal jumps up and runs out of the yard.

'The song … the song,' Rasik cries.

'Bother the song. I'm off to eat kul berries.'

'Na … na.' Kamini runs after her. 'Come back, you foolish girl. Don't you know what people are saying about you?' Then, turning to the smiling Rasik, she asks angrily, 'Is this something to be merry about, Mahanto?'

Rasik sways his stork neck from side to side and sings in a high quavering voice.

Rai Kamalini unfurls her petals; black bee Krishna hovers near.
People taunt and slander her.
She does not care; she knows no fear.

*

Ranjan, the headman's son, was a couple of years older than Kamal. As children, playing 'House House' under the banyan tree, he would insist on being Kamal's husband. A scene from the past:

Half lying on the spreading roots, Ranjan mops his forehead and calls out in the voice of a seasoned householder, 'Bou! O Bou! Light my hookah and fan me for a while. It's so hot…'

'A ha ha ha!' Kamal makes faces at him from behind her veil. 'As if I have nothing better to do! Light your hookah yourself...'

'Mind your language, woman,' Ranjan roars at her. 'Remember that a sun-scorched peasant and a burning coulter are equally deadly. Another word from you and I'll break your bones.'

Kamal marches up to him and thrusts her bare back under his nose. 'Break my bones,' she dares him. 'Let's see what a big man you are!'

Ranjan takes up the challenge. Twisting her thick braid with one hand he deals half-a-dozen blows on her back with the other. Whereupon Kamal picks up a handful of dust and, flinging it in Ranjan's face, bursts into a fit of weeping. 'How dare you hit me?' she howls, her face red and streaked with tears.

Soft-hearted Bhola stands up for her. 'It's only a game Ranjan,' he says. 'You shouldn't have hit her.'

'Hmph! I'm her husband. What sort of man will stand by quietly when his wife humiliates him?'

'Husband!' Kamal lashes out at him between sobs. 'What sort of husband are you? Useless as a provider. Only fit to beat me and order me about. Jah! Jah! I won't be your wife anymore. And I won't talk to you ever again.'

'Don't cry, Kamli.' Bhola takes her hand tenderly in his. 'I'll be your husband.'

'And I'll be your wife.' Pari, the grocer's daughter, looks up adoringly into Ranjan's face.

'No, Pari.' Ranjan shakes his head gravely. 'I'm not getting married again.'

Kamal looks up. She stops crying and, withdrawing her hand from Bhola's, moves slowly towards Ranjan.

'Take care,' Bhola calls out a warning. 'He'll beat you again.'

Kamal sighs, assuming the weary voice and manner of the married women she saw around her all the time, then says, 'Well. He may beat me or love me. It is his will. After all I married him and a woman, however ill-treated, cannot marry twice—can she?'

The game resumes. Kamal beats her forehead with a tiny hand and sighs, 'There's no rice in the house. No salt. No oil. But does my husband care? Radhe! Radhe! What a worthless man I've married! Does he expect me to go out and earn money and buy the provisions myself?'

At this, a faint smile appears on Ranjan's gloomy countenance. He moves to Kamal's side and whispers in her ear, 'I won't beat you again, Bou. Never again. I promise.'

Today Ranjan is a strapping youth. His eyes are tinged with the awakening of a dewy morn in spring. And Kamal is a lotus bud on the verge of bloom. It will take her a while longer to unfurl her thousand petals. But the promise is in the air. It is visible in the slight halting of her dancing footsteps and the shy mist creeping into her flashing, bird-wing eyes. She's still wild and restless as a forest doe. Yet a veil of restraint, fine as gossamer, is perceived in her words and movements…

Reaching the kul tree Ranjan clambered up the trunk and proceeded to shake the branches. *Tup tup tup* the berries dropped like rain. Kamal ran this way and that collecting them. '*O Ma!*' she exclaimed, biting into one, 'this must be the sweetest kul I've ever tasted.'

'Don't eat it all.' Ranjan jumped to the ground. 'Give me the rest.' Then, chewing on the half-eaten berry, he smiled at his companion. 'It's as sweet as sweet can be. That's because you bit into it first.'

'Haribol! Is my mouth made of sugar?'

'Hunh. You're my sugar.'

'And you're my pepper.' Kamal giggled. Then, sobering down, she added, 'Do you realize what you've just done? You've lost your caste.'

'I don't care a crow's leg for my caste.' Ranjan took her hand in his. 'I'll happily become a Vaishnav if you marry me.'

'Arre! Arre!' Kamal snatched her hand away and ran home. But she kept looking back at him, her face glowing with joy.

Ranjan's mother loved Kamal for her pretty face and winsome ways and gave her a share of the sweets and toys she bought for Ranjan. But on that day her love changed into intense hate. '*Daini! Haramjadi!*' she screamed curses at the absent girl. 'Wait till I catch you. I'll give you such a lashing with my broom! And where's that good-for-nothing boy? *O Ma!* What'll I do now? My caste is lost and...'

'*Chup*, woman, *chup*!' her husband cautioned in an undertone. 'Stop screaming your head off. If the truth gets known in the village we'll be thrown out of our clan. We'll be ruined.'

For, the kul-eating incident hadn't gone unnoticed. There was an eyewitness. A person no other than the headman, Ranjan's father.

Ranjan walked in nonchalantly a few minutes later. '*O re O mukhpora*!' was his mother's loving greeting. 'Have you taken leave of your senses? What were you thinking of ... you scum of my womb?'

'Serve my meal,' Ranjan growled. 'I've come home because I'm hungry. Not to listen to abuses.'

His mother's face twisted with disgust. 'Hasn't Kamli's half-eaten berry filled your stomach? Well then, I'll fill it. I'll stuff your mouth with ashes hot from the hearth.'

The fire in Ranjan's eyes died out. Hanging his head he stared at the floor.

'You should have died the moment you were born,' his father's voice hissed in his ear. 'But I know how to deal with wayward sons. I'll cast you off without one paisa. I'll drive you out of the house…' He stormed away with a furious clacking of khadams.

'I've decided to get you married next month.' The mother tried to soften the blow. 'I'll find a girl so beautiful—Kamli will be nothing to her.'

'No.'

'No?'

'I'm not marrying anyone else. I've decided to become a Vaishnav.'

The mother stared at him speechless with shock. Then, flinging all caution to the winds, she screamed in panic. '*O go!* Come back. Come back. Hear what your son just said…'

*

'Mahanto!' Ranjan called from the bamboo gate of Rasa Kunja. This was a place where all manner of men, young and old, rich and poor, Vaishnav and non-Vaishnav, congregated. Rasik Das was a good host. The young ones could smoke as much tobacco as they wanted. The elders opted for ganja.

'Ah!' Rasik exclaimed. 'It's Raikamal's Ranjan at my door!' Then, peering sharply into the boy's face he said, 'You look hungry.'

'I am. Can I eat with you?'

'You can. But you'll lose your caste.'

'I don't care. I'm becoming a Vaishnav.'

The old man nodded and smiled. Wagging his beard he began humming a song…

Faith, honour and line I held not dear. At thy feet I lie … a slave

'*Dhat*!' Ranjan cried, blushing furiously. 'What's wrong with you?'

'Rasik's heart is filled with joy. Joy that knows no bounds. It is spilling over in song.'

'Stop your nonsense and listen to me. I want to become a Vaishnav. Will you initiate me?'

'If Raikamal tells me to, I will.'

'Why? Is Kamli your lawyer?'

Rasik swayed his head, a mysterious smile on his lips. Ranjan waited for a few minutes. 'Very well. I'll go and ask her myself.' He stomped off in a huff.

Kamal was sitting under the flowering creepers of Kamal Kunja, sorting through a pile of berries, when Bhola tiptoed in and took her hand. 'Let go of me, you dolt!' Kamal giggled and tried to pull her fingers away. But Bhola wouldn't let her.

'Kamli,' he whispered, his voice charged with emotion. Kamal took a handful of berries with her other hand and squashed them against his face. *Hee! Hee! Hee!* The sight of the boy, his cheeks, chin and nose spattered with kul pulp, sent her into gales of laughter.

'Sugar!' Ranjan's voice called softly from the wattle hedge.

'Oh! It's my pepper!' Kamal exclaimed. But the sound of Ranjan's voice struck terror in Bhola's heart. He jumped up and ran out of the akhara.

'Come back, Bhola!' Kamal ran after him. 'Why do you run away?' Ranjan took in the scene with lowering brows and, turning his face, strode rapidly in the other direction. Kamal was puzzled and cried out to him to return but he didn't look back, leave alone reply. This infuriated the girl. 'Go wherever you like,' she shouted after both of them. 'I don't care one bit. I'm no one's slave.'

That evening, Ranjan's father burst into Kamal Kunja. 'We both have children,' he cried, clutching Kamini's hands in his. 'Give mine back to me.'

'What do you mean?'

'Ranjan says he will not marry anyone else. He will become a Vaishnav.'

Kamini's face paled. 'If indeed it has gone so far,' she murmured uneasily, 'can I break my daughter's heart?'

'I'll give you two bighas of land. And … and money.'

'*Chhi!* Is my Kamli's happiness on sale?'

Suddenly there was a loud thud as of something heavy falling to the ground. Kamini ran to the door. Kamal stood outside, her sari soaking wet, the mud pot in which she had fetched water lying in shards at her feet. Her face was white and she was shaking like a leaf.

Kamini put her arms around the girl. 'Never mind the pot,' she said. 'Come inside and change your sari.' As mother and daughter entered the door a shadow slipped past them. It was the headman.

'Ma,' Kamal said after a while. 'Some people from our village are going to Nabadweep for the Raas festival. Why don't we go too?'

'Y … yes. We could go … I suppose.'

Kamal sprang up and ran out of the house. 'Where are you going?' Kamini called after her.

'To fetch Stork Babaji. He must come with us.'

Kamal was back within minutes, dragging Rasik by the hand. He looked puzzled but didn't ask any questions.

'An excellent idea,' he said, falling in with Kamini's plans at once. 'We'll leave tomorrow at dawn.'

*

Reaching Nabadweep, Kamini bought an akhara and made it neat and comfortable. The garden she planted with flowering bushes and vines. And, every evening, she invited the local

Vaishnavs to hold discourses and sing kirtan. Rasik was charmed by the young men and women who came to the akhara. 'Aa ha ha ha!' he exclaimed, 'my eyes have never beheld such beauty before! This land is blessed. Haven't our Mahaprabhu's feet touched every inch of this ground? Isn't the air still redolent with his breath?'

'Aa ha ha ha!' Kamal mimicked, doubling over with laughter. 'My Stork Babaji is feeling the need of a Vaishnavi at last! Choose one from the beauties here and hang a garland around her neck as fast as you can.'

The days went by. The evening gatherings in the akhara swelled with more and more young men hovering like bees around a newly opening lotus. But Kamal seemed unaware of them. She lived in her own world and thought her own thoughts. She wasn't pensive or withdrawn. She laughed and chatted with all but chose no one for special attention.

'Kamalini!' Subal, the fairest and most perfectly formed of all the Vaishnav youths, came upon her one morning. 'You seem lost in your thoughts. Won't you share them with me?'

Kamal looked up. 'It's mid-morning,' she said. 'I was wondering why my Subal Sakha hasn't come to me on his way to the pasture.'

Subal trembled at her words. Seizing her hands he murmured in a voice choked with emotion. 'Sakhi … sakhi…'

Kamal disengaged them gently and murmured, 'Is this conduct becoming of my beautiful Subal Sakha?'

Hurt and embarrassed, Subal turned to leave but Kamal stopped him, 'Why do you go away? You are my friend, are you not?'

Weeks passed into months. The year was almost over. But Kamini refused to leave Nabadweep. 'Why go back?' she asked wearily whenever Rasik proposed returning to the village, 'isn't it better that we spend our last days in this holy land and die breathing the air of the Ganga?'

The lotus bud, in the meanwhile, had burst into bloom; her thousand petals quivering with life. She no longer tossed and danced in the unruly wind. She floated serenely on the ripples, sending eddies of perfume into the air. Rasik gazed at her in wonder. Sometimes he sang snatches of an old Vaishnav love song…

Kamini was able to fulfil her last wish. She died in Nabadweep. She didn't suffer much. Just four days of fever. 'The thought of death doesn't sadden me, Mahanto,' she said. 'I'm filled with bliss at the thought of leaving my mortal remains in Ma Ganga's lap. At Gourango's feet. Only…'

'Why do you talk of death? What's wrong with you?'

'Nothing. Yet everything. I feel I'm going far … very far away. But one thought pulls me back. My daughter…'

'If it comes to that,' Rasik's eyes glittered with tears, 'I'll take care of Kamal.'

Kamini sighed. 'I knew that, Mahanto. Still … I wanted an assurance.'

'Ma!' A sobbing Kamal flung herself on her mother's breast. Kamini placed a trembling hand on the girl's head. 'Don't weep, child. Parents don't live forever. Promise me…'

'What is it, Ma?'

'The creeper that doesn't cling to a tree lies, weak and vulnerable, on the ground. It has no strength. Animals nibble at it…' Her voice choked on the words.

'I know. I give you my word … I'll marry.'

'Don't take a son away from his parents.'

'I won't.'

'Jai Radhe! Radhe!' Rasik cried, making sure his voice reached Kamini's ears.

'Gobindo … Gobindo,' the dying lips murmured.

*

Time, like a mother, sings an unending lullaby that erases memory and soothes the suffering mortal into a state of blessed oblivion. The pain of loss eased with every passing day. Kamal laughed once more. And her laughter found an echo in the old man's breast.

'Raikamal,' he ventured one day. But he seemed unable to go on.

'What is it?' Kamal was surprised. 'Why don't you speak? Do you have a fishbone stuck in your throat?'

Rasik swallowed, then making a great effort, blurted out. 'It has to do with your marriage.'

Kamal's face paled. 'I understand,' she answered softly. Then, looking up at the sky, she muttered, 'The day is almost done, Mahanto. Let us wait for the night.' Rising she went into her room and locked the door. Weeping bitterly, she called out to the One she believed to be her true friend and guide. 'Gobindo! Gobindo! My heart and mind are another's. To whom shall I give this empty shell?' But all she received in reply was a chilling silence. Abandoned even by her God the bereft girl sought the answer herself. *She had to deceive someone. Who would it be?* Faces came and went before her eyes.

Rasik was sitting in the yard when Kamal came to him, the red gold of the setting sun glowing in her cheeks. 'We'll need flowers for the garlands, Mahanto,' she said.

'I'll go at once.' Rasik rose to his feet.

He returned in a while, his dhuti dripping wet, holding a sheaf of lotus buds in his arms. 'Raikamal,' he called out to her happily, 'I've brought lotus as befits…'

Kamal came and stood before him. The rest of the sentence died in his throat. She wore a tussar sari with a deep red border. Her hair hung loose down her back like a rippling river and the caste marks of her sect were etched in sandal paste on her delicate nose and brow. He had never seen her look so beautiful.

'Change your dhuti,' she said. 'Wear the one I've kept in your room.' Kamal took the flowers and began stringing them into a garland. 'You string one too, Mahanto.'

'A good idea. I'll fetch Subal as soon as the garlands are done.'

Their task completed, the two rose to their feet. Kamal slipped her garland over Rasik's head and said, 'Won't you give me yours?' Taking up the bowl of sandal paste she adorned his wrinkled forehead.

'You throw away a silver rupee,' Rasik said sadly, 'and tie a copper pie in your anchal. Is that wise, Raikamal?'

'Copper and gold are often mistaken for one another. I've found gold.'

Rasik smiled and placed his garland around Kamal's neck.

Rasik decorated the bed with flowers that night, strewing the brightest, freshest blooms on one side and wilting, decaying ones on the other. 'You and me,' he said.

'Yes.' Kamal lowered herself on the withered side. 'The fresh flowers are yours, Mahanto—the stale ones mine.' Her laughter rang out like a peal of bells. Rasik took up a lamp and held the light to Kamal's face. He gazed at her so intently—it seemed as though his eyes would never have their fill. 'The more I see you,' he murmured, 'the greater my awe and wonder! Radharani works in inscrutable ways but her bounty is immeasurable.'

Kamal lay on the wilted flowers, her eyes hard and dry. Rasik, on the other side, slept peacefully. Around midnight, she felt herself being drawn to the old man's breast. His shrivelled arms had the strength of a crazed elephant, his skeletal fingers the tensile grip of a hangman's rope. Kamal was frightened. 'Mahanto! Mahanto!' she shrieked fearfully…

The arrival of dawn saw Rasik sitting in the yard motionless as a statue. His limbs were still, his eyes fixed. It seemed as though he had stopped breathing. Kamal's heart melted. She wanted to comfort him but couldn't find the words.

'Kamal.' It was Rasik who broke the silence. Kamal looked up in surprise. Why had he called her Kamal? A strange feeling came over her. She felt slighted, diminished. 'Kamal,' he said again. 'I'm made of flesh and blood.'

'We all are. But, today, you've turned yourself to stone.'

'Yes. Yes … like Ahalya.'

'Tear off this garland of embers, Mahanto,' Kamal said softly. 'Free yourself from this curse.'

'I tried to escape last night but couldn't. My feet were willing but my eyes wouldn't leave your face. This … this shame is my burden and I must carry it. But don't abandon me,' he gripped her hands and pleaded. 'Don't leave me … ever.'

'Then let's go somewhere else.' Kamal wiped her streaming face. 'Some place faraway.'

'Where?'

'Vrindavan.'

'No … no!' A shiver passed over the ancient frame. 'I cannot show this face, blackened with shame, to the moon of Brajadham.'

'Why, Mahanto? Is loving me such a great sin?'

There was no answer.

'Very well. We'll have no destination … no home. We'll wander aimlessly from village to village seeking alms on our way. The open sky will be our roof and the shade of trees our resting place.'

The stone statue quivered into life. 'Let's go then.' He rose to his feet.

Stepping out into the open, Rasik heaved a sigh of relief. He could inhale the fragrance of the lotus beside him but its tender stem wasn't fastened around his neck like a noose.

Leaving Nabadweep behind, the two walked mile after mile till, hungry and footsore, they stopped by a pond at the edge of a village. 'I'll take a dip and cook a meal,' Kamal said like a seasoned housewife, 'but there's no salt in the bundle, Mahanto. Go into the village and buy some.'

Rasik returned an hour later to find Kamal sitting before a fire of twigs, stirring rice in a clay pot. Her long, wet hair was drawn to the top of her head in a knot. The ridge of her nose and gleaming forehead were etched in sandal paste. A group of people stood around her staring and nudging one another.

'What a beauty! Who is she?'

'She doesn't seem to belong to these parts.'

'What is your name, Vaishnavi?' One of the men addressed her directly. 'Where do you live?'

Kamal didn't deign to reply. But Rasik stepped forward. 'Her name is Raikamal,' he announced. 'She lives in Rasa Kunja.'

'Where did this one spring up from? Who on earth are you?'

'I'm the husband! The Vaishnavi's Vaishnav. My name is Aayaan Ghosh.' His lips twitched in a smile.

The crowd melted away. Rasik twanged his ektara softly and hummed a love song.

Days passed. The two walked, apparently without direction, but whether it was from the twists and turns of the road or the hidden promptings of the two hearts, they arrived one afternoon, at the gate of Rasa Kunja. Tears sprang to Rasik's eyes as he saw the ruin that had once been his beloved akhara. Kamal Kunja hadn't fared any better. The walls had crumbled to the ground; the thatch blown away. But the bower stood intact, its canopy effulgent with blooms.

'I'm glad to be home, Mahanto.' Kamal lay down on the fallen flowers. 'I don't want to leave … ever.'

'Neither do I. The sky, air and earth of my native village are tying me with unseen bonds. Only…' Rasik hesitated a little, 'you must let me live in Rasa Kunja.'

'So you shall, Mahanto. So you shall. Rest assured. I won't disturb you with my presence.'

'But I shall come to you. We'll swing together under the clouds on Jhulan. I shall adorn you with flowers on Raas and sprinkle saffron and kumkum on your face on Dol.'

'You've thought of all the leelas. What about the difficult one? The bearing of Govardhan mountain?

'That will be my first task. From tomorrow morning I'll begin repairing the walls and thatching the roof of Kamal Kunja. But now let's go to the village and collect some alms.'

The two went from door to door greeting old acquaintances and filling their satchels with rice. Reaching the headman's house, Rasik's steps faltered. 'We have enough for today,' he muttered uneasily.

'But this is where my pepper lives,' Kamal cried gaily. 'He'll be hurt if I don't stop at his door…'

Rasik glanced at her face. It was as radiant as the moon. Rasik felt a stab of jealousy ripping his chest. His eyes burned with tears he dared not shed. Forcing a smile on his wan lips he twanged the string of his ektara, blending it with Kamal's high sweet voice. 'Radhe Krishna! I've come for some alms, Ma!'

A young woman opened the door. From the ghomta on her head and the sindoor on her brow and parting it was obvious that she was the daughter-in-law of the house. 'Sing a song, Vaishnavi,' she demanded. The proud tilt of her head and the sparkle in her eyes told Kamal that she was a happy, fulfilled woman. She hadn't been denied her husband's love...

*

Rasik's hard work turned Kamal Kunja into the serene, beautiful akhara it had been during Kamini's time. Kirtan was sung every evening. Kamal's childhood friends, Bhola, Binod and Panchanan came. Only Ranjan stayed away. 'I've requested him so many times,' Bhola grumbled, 'but he says...'

'What does he say?'

'Leave it. It isn't meant for your ears.'

Kamal saw the compassion in Bhola's eyes. 'Tell me,' she insisted, 'I want to know...'

'He said ... *to look on her face is a sin.*' Seeing the tears gather in the girl's eyes he added tenderly, 'Shall I speak to him again?'

'*Chhi!*'

A few days later, Ranjan saw her at the bathing ghat. She had just stepped out of the water. Her wet sari clung to the curves of her exquisite form. Her face, framed by her long waving hair, was like a dew-drenched lotus. Ranjan couldn't tear his eyes away.

'Sugar,' he called imperiously.

Kamal looked up. A tall powerfully built man stood before her. His arms were tense with muscles, his chest a stone wall. Kamal's eyes dimmed. Was this the tender youth she had known and loved? Her heart was torn with pity at his lost innocence. With the keen instinct of a woman in love she looked into his soul. She searched long and deep but found not a trace of light. It was a hollow shell, dark and empty.

Ranjan came and stood by her. So close, she could feel his fevered breath licking her cool, wave-washed body. She remembered her bridal night. The terror of Rasik's arms coiling and writhing about her limbs like snakes, his bloodshot eyes gazing into hers ... Picking up her waterpot Kamal walked away in the opposite direction. *I had so little left*, she thought sadly, *even that little has been taken from me. With what shall I sustain myself?*

'Mahanto!' Ranjan called loudly from the gate of Kamal Kunja that evening. Kamal started up. Dropping her cymbals she ran into her room. Rasik's love song froze in his throat. *This is the beginning of the end*, he thought, glancing at the sinking sun. A few minutes later he stood outside the girl's door. 'Raikamal,' he called, 'Ranjan is here to see you.'

'I can't come out. I have a headache.'

'*Chhi!* What will he think? Is he not your best friend?'

'I beg you, Mahanto,' Kamal burst into tears. 'Don't torture me with your kindness. I'm a weak woman. I cannot bear the weight of your love.'

'Listen to me, Kamal.'

'Leave me alone for tonight. I'll hear all you have to say tomorrow.'

'Tomorrow might be too late.'

'So be it. As of this moment let all words cease between us.'

'Shall I stroke your forehead and make the pain go away?'

'No! No! No!'

Rasik turned. Leaving the door open he walked out of Kamal Kunja. The sky above his head was dark and starless. The night was silent. Only a faint moaning of the trees echoed Kamal's pain. A sound unheard. Only sensed...

Ranjan tiptoed in through the door Rasik had left open. *Sin is like a snake. It lives in a secret hole and creeps out in the darkness of night*. 'Sugar' ... his whisper entered Kamal's ear like the deadly hiss of a forked tongue. She sprang up with a shudder and ran out of the akhara, not stopping till she reached Rasa Kunja. Her clothes and hair were dishevelled; her eyes wide with terror. 'Mahanto! Mahanto!' she called and banged on the door till it opened. Rasik stood within.

'Are you happy, Raikamal?' he asked gently.

'Ranjan came...'

'You ... sent him away?' A smile, like a shaft of moonlight, blew away the clouds from Rasik's face. But Kamal noticed that his hands were shaking and he was having trouble articulating his words.

'What have you done to yourself?' she cried out fearfully.

'Poison! Ranjan and you ... I couldn't bear the thought ... death was preferable. But now ... now that you are here ... I want to live. Save me Raikamal ... save me!'

'*Ma go!*' Kamal shrieked. 'What will become of me? My sin...'

'The sin was mine. You are Raikamal. You're cast in Radharani's mould. Can sin touch you? Oof!' His face was contorted with agony. Foam gathered at his lips.

The night waned. The sky pearled with the first touch of dawn. Kamal sat outside the door of Rasa Kunja with Rasik's limp body in her lap...

*

Rasik's mortal remains find a resting place under the blossom-laden bower of Kamal Kunja. Kamal lights a lamp there, every evening, and sings the songs he loved. Her friends come to see her. Only Ranjan does not come.

'Shall I bring him?' Bhola asks.

'He'll come on his own ... someday.'

An elderly Vaishnavi says to her, 'We are going to Vrindavan. Why don't you come with us?'

'No. I've had my fill of pilgrimages. I'm happy where I am.'

'Gobindo! Gobindo!' The woman touches her ears. 'What Vaishnavi will throw away the chance to go to Brajadham? The village women are right. You're a harlot.'

Kamal smiles and sings:

They call me a harlot; I'm in love with the name, dear friend.
Spurning it ... shall I lose my beloved Shyam?
Radha comes before Shyam. They cry out ... Radheshyam!

Lighting a lamp at the mound covered with madhavi and malati flowers she touches her brow to the ground and murmurs ... *guru... guru ... guru.*

Motho's Daughter

Kalyani Thakur Charal

The night has waned, O Shuk and Shari
Rise from your love nest and tweet
A wake-up call with the mother of peace
For Sri Hari ... the moon-like one.

A bitterly cold dawn in the middle of winter. Bibhavati croons softly as she goes about her work. She has lit a fire of husks and set a large wok of paddy on the boil. She wears only a khadi shawl to protect her from the cold. But the smouldering husk keeps her limbs warm and dry.

Nishikanta slaves from morning till night but takes care to wake up at dawn to feed the cow. Picking up the pieces of straw that have fallen from Bibhavati's bundle he goes to the cowshed and drops them in the feeding trough. Then, as one continues to boil the paddy the other tends to the cow.

If you are poor the only one you can call out to, when in trouble, is God...

'Never forget Thakur's advice.' Nishikanta turns to his wife. 'Starve if you have to. But don't neglect to give your children an education. That is His fervent wish.' With a cautionary glance at his wife, he goes back to his work. Bibhavati nods in complete agreement.

Nishikanta and his wife belong to a sect of Krishna worshippers who call themselves Motho. The term, corrupted by frequent usage to Motho, was originally Mattwa, meaning 'possessed of divine frenzy'. Mothos value learning above everything else. Nishikanta quotes this passage, exhorting the community to educate their children, at least once every day. Bibhavati, too, is a passionate advocate of the cause.

Bibhavati has scoured a portion of the yard and swabbed it with cow dung. It is clean and dry. The paddy is done too. Bibhavati lifts the enormous wok by its ears and scatters the contents on the smooth surface. Clouds of steam rises from the freshly parboiled rice and the air is heavy with its fragrance. After it cools, she will stamp it with her feet to loosen the husks.

Birds have started leaving their nests. Bibhavati can hear them calling out to each other from the garden next door. A cock crows lustily from another house. It seems to come from a vast distance. There is a machan supported by bamboo stilts in one corner of Bibhavati's yard in which her ducks are penned for the night. Startled by these early-morning sounds, they flap their wings in alarm. Feathers rustle and loud quacks are heard.

Bibhavati stirs cow dung in a pail of water and sprinkles it on the rest of the yard. It looks clean, she had swabbed it only yesterday morning, but she knows that the children have urinated on it at night. The clean sweet smell of cow dung will drive away the foul odour. She does another thing. She fills a basket with ashes from her cooking pit and pours it into the open latrine. She does this every morning. She does all this plus much more, day after day, month after month, year after year.

Nishikanta toils in the fields and does other jobs as well. He cleans the cowshed, milks the cow and takes it out to graze day after day, month after month, year after year. The work is hard and tedious.

Is it to relieve the dreary monotony that husband and wife have turned to religion? Do they frequent Hari Sabhas and Mahotsavs to forget, if only for a little while, their lifeless, colourless, bleak, arid existence?

If so, where is the harm? And even if, while reciting Hari's name and joining the refrain in kirtans, they convey their joys and sorrows to the Lord or seek his help with the family finances and the welfare of their children ... there is nothing wrong with that surely?

However, singing paeans in praise of the Lord and uttering his name a hundred times is not enough for Mothos these days. Reading passages from holy books has become the fashion at religious meetings. Bibhavati's education had been sketchy to begin with. But whatever little learning she had picked up in the *pathshala* of her parental village would have soon been forgotten if it wasn't for these books. After the reciting and singing are over, Bibhavati reads a chapter from some religious text by the dim light of a hurricane lamp.

*

'Sing a song, Geeta,' Ashwini Gosain prompts.

Geeta has a good singing voice. She and a few other girls frequent the Hari Sabhas and sing there.

Geeta begins her song...

O Hari! Friend and beloved
Reveal thyself and grant me eternal life

Bibhavati tries hard to drown herself in Geeta's song. To immerse herself in love of Krishna. But other thoughts come teeming into her mind. Her younger son has failed her. He has given up studies and fallen into bad company. He has taken to drink. This sorrow has swept away all the joys of her life. She spends hours every morning and evening in puja. She changes the water in the holy pot every Wednesday. She bathes the idol with her tears. Yet…

Why? she asks her beloved Hari, over and over again. She and her husband have led exemplary lives. They have obeyed the commands of the Lord to the letter. *But has He dispensed justice?*

She recites from the *Hari Lila Amrit* every day. Yet she knows no peace. Fear and anxiety for her child dispel all other thoughts. *What will he do? How will he make a living?* Worry eats into her like a canker. She voices this fear wherever she goes.

Nishikanta has more strength of mind. He is able to internalize sorrow and not show it. He carries out his daily tasks faithfully and meticulously. Without complaint.

The boy comes home drunk every night. He storms and shouts. Sometimes he vomits. Bibhavati can't bear this blow to her hopes. She falls into a decline. She becomes so ill that no doctor can save her…

*

With Bibhavati's passing, Nishikanta's world crashed around him. There was no one left to look after his household. Bibhavati had worked day and night but never let go of her primary principle in life. To exhort her children to study. But despite all her efforts she had failed with one. The others had cleared their exams, found jobs and established themselves. The only one left at home was the problem son.

Nishikanta decided to get him married. With a daughter-in-law in the house some sense of normality would return. She might, with Hari's blessings, even guide her husband and bring him back to the right path. He found a girl from his own community. She had little education. Nishikanta was disappointed but how could he expect a better match for a worthless boy like his son?

The daughter-in-law came and took charge of the house. She was a good girl. Pious and hardworking. She rose at dawn every day, finished her cleaning and other chores, then bathed and went to the puja room. She performed the rites with meticulous care and devotion, then entered the kitchen. She took pains to cook a fine meal every day. Within a year she gave birth to a son, then after another year … another. Nishikanta's house started bearing a festive look. Puja was performed with fanfare every day and meals became more and more elaborate. But Nishikanta wasn't happy. Because the one thing she did not do was to teach her children the value of education and exhort them to study.

The boys were sent to school at the appropriate time. But they were careless and lazy and hated studies. Within a few years they followed in their father's footsteps and dropped out of school.

Nishikanta had grown old and feeble by now. He couldn't do the work he had done before. He disliked the atmosphere of the house so much that he moved out of it and started sleeping in the bamboo machan that had housed the ducks in Bibhavati's time. 'The girl cares more about puja and good food than the upbringing of her children,' he was heard to mutter from time to time. And when Bibhavati's absence became unbearable and he fell into a state of total despair, he beat his chest and shouted so loud … everyone could hear him. 'What have I done, O

Thakur! What sort of Motho's daughter have I brought home as a bride for my son? She doesn't listen to me. No one listens to me. I have lost everything. I'm a ruined man...'

Abhagi's Heaven

Saratchandra Chattopadhyay

Only seven days of fever and Thakurdas Mukhopadhyay's wife passed away. Old Mukhopadhyay Moshai, grown extremely wealthy from a flourishing business in rice and paddy, had four sons and three daughters—all with children of their own. Sons-in-law, grandchildren, neighbours and servants filled the rooms in a measure that befitted not a house of death but of jubilation. Men, women and children from the entire village crowded at the gates in the hope of catching a glimpse of the splendid funeral procession which would accompany the dead woman to her final resting place. Her weeping daughters lined her parting with sindoor and covered her feet with alta. Her daughters-in-law dressed her in a resplendent new sari and adorned her brow with sandal paste. Then, wiping the last traces of dust from her feet with their sari ends, touched them reverently to their foreheads. Flowers, garlands and basil leaves, clouds of fragrant incense smoke and the resounding clamour and bustle turned the day of mourning into a joyous replica of the one, fifty years ago, when the mistress of the great house had first set out on her ceremonial journey as a little bride of ten, to her husband's home.

Bidding a last farewell to his companion of nearly a lifetime, old Mukhopadhyay Moshai dashed the tears away from his eyes with a surreptitious hand and, assuming a serene expression, tried to comfort the weeping women.

And now the magnificent cortège started on its way to deafening cries of *Bolo Hari, Hari Bol!* As soon as it left the gates the assembled crowd of villagers scrambled after it. Only one woman hung back. She had stood apart from the rest all this while and now she followed fearfully, keeping a discreet distance from the others. This pale shadowy creature was Kangali's mother.

She had been on her way to the weekly haat with a few aubergines she had picked from the bushes outside her hut when the marvellous spectacle caught her eyes, leaving her spellbound. She forgot the aubergines bundled in a corner of her sari. Forgotten, too, were her hopes of selling them and returning home with a few coins. Wiping away the tears from her streaming eyes, she followed the crowd to the cremation ghat that stood on a bank of the Garud.

Standing on a mound, a little way off, she looked on with eager eyes at the huge wooden logs, stacks of sandalwood, ghee, honey, camphor and incense that lay beside the bier. She dared not go any closer. She was an untouchable, a duley by caste. Even her shadow was shunned by the others.

She looked on stoically as the preliminary rituals were being performed but when the body was lowered on the wide platform, she could hold herself in no longer. A sob tore through her throat as a wild desire rose in her. She wanted to rush towards the alta-covered feet and touch them to her brow. Curbing the impulse with difficulty she gazed at the scene before her eyes. How beautiful it was! The high-born lady in her priceless sari, her parting covered with sindoor and her fair feet smothered in alta! *A ha ha ha*. Abhagi suppressed a sigh as Mukhopadhyay Moshai's eldest son took up the bunch of flaming jute stalks, purified by the chants of the priests, and touched them to his mother's lips to tumultuous cries of *Bolo Hari, Hari Bol* rising from hundreds of throats.

Kangali's mother was so moved that tears poured down her cheeks. *Ma*, she called out to the dead woman without words. *What great good fortune is yours! You are on your journey to Heaven leaving behind a grieving husband, sons and daughters, grandchildren, kinsmen, dependents and servants. You are a queen and I a lowly creature not fit to touch your feet. Still, waft a blessing towards me before you go. Grace me with the boon that I too, like you, may receive my last fire from Kangali's hands.*

Fire from a son's hand! Her limbs trembled with ecstasy at the thought. Ah! The beauty of it. The glory of it! Her breast heaved with powerful feelings.

Standing on the mound Kangali's mother strained her eyes on the newly lit pyre from which a column of smoke was rising, spiralling towards the sky. It stung her eyes rendering her vision blurred and hazy, playing tricks with it. She saw a tiny chariot, she could swear to it, at the tip of the bluish grey swirl just where it met the sky. Exotic images were etched in gold on the sides. The crest was entwined with flowering vines. There was someone sitting within. She could not see her face clearly but recognized her easily from the wide parting filled with sindoor; the feet covered with alta. She gazed at the woman in awe and adoration.

'Ma!' She felt a tug at her sari. A boy of about fourteen stood by her side looking at her with bewildered eyes. 'Why are you standing here? When will you do the cooking?'

'I will, in a while, son. Look!' She pointed to the sky. 'Can you see the chariot? Our chaste and holy mistress, our Bamun Ma, is sitting in it. It is taking her to Heaven.'

'What chariot? Where?' Kangali's eyes turned to the pointing finger. 'That's smoke,' he said dismissively, 'smoke from the pyre. You've gone crazy, Ma.' Then, pouting like a child, he muttered, 'It's hours past noon. Don't you know I am hungry?' Seeing his mother's eyes fill up with tears, he added, 'Why do you weep because the Brahmin lady is dead? What is she to you?'

Now Kangali's mother came to her senses. She realized how foolish it was to stand for hours in the cremation ground shedding tears over someone else's death when her own son went hungry. Besides, a mother's tears brought bad luck to her children. Drying her cheeks with a furtive hand she tried to smile, 'Why should I weep, son? My eyes are watering from the smoke and...'

'Watering from the smoke indeed! You were crying.'

The mother fell silent. Taking Kangali's hand she climbed down the bank and took a few dips in the river. Making her son do the same she returned home with him. A small sigh escaped her. She would have liked to watch the beautiful ceremony to the end. But the needs of her son came first.

*

Parents are often injudicious in their choice of names for their children. The Creator smiles at their foolishness and dismisses it with the contempt it deserves. But sometimes He is angered and decides to teach the inane mortal a lesson. Then the name so carelessly given turns into a symbol of the innocent child's fate. From birth to death, she hears her name ringing in her ears; jeering, mocking, reminding her of what she can expect.

Kangali's mother was a young woman. She hadn't lived long in the world. But she had spent her years, few as they were, tottering under the weight of her name and its implications. Her mother had died in giving her birth. Her father, enraged at the bereavement of which she was the cause, had named her Abhagi—the ill-fated one.

Hers had been a childhood with no mother and a father who spent all his time fishing in the river and hobnobbing with his friends with never a thought for the little girl left at home. Yet the tiny creature had not only survived but also grown to womanhood and, in course of time, given birth to Kangali. The man who had married her went by the name of Rasik Bagh. But Bagh, the tiger, liked another tigress and one fine day he picked up his things and moved to the village in which she lived, leaving Abhagi alone with her infant son.

That son was now in his fifteenth year. He had just started learning to weave bamboo slips into mats and baskets. Abhagi yearned for the day when he would be earning enough to support them both. 'Just another year or so,' she told herself frequently, her heart lifting at the thought, 'and my troubles will be over…'

*

Kangali ate his meal and went to the pond to wash his hands and rinse his mouth. Returning, he was surprised to see his mother putting away the leftovers in an earthen bowl.

'Why, Ma!' he cried out. 'Aren't you going to eat?'

'The day is almost done,' Abhagi muttered. 'I'm not hungry anymore.'

'*Hunh!*' Kangali snorted in disbelief. 'Not hungry anymore! You haven't kept anything for yourself. That's the truth. Isn't it?'

It was a trick Abhagi often played when there wasn't enough food for them both. Kangali knew it. He insisted on examining the rice pot and found there was enough left for one person. And now, convinced that she really wasn't hungry, he smiled contentedly and came and sat in her lap. It was an odd thing for a boy of fourteen to do, but Kangali had been sickly for a large part of his infancy and boyhood and Abhagi had kept him physically close. Unable to romp and frolic with other boys he derived all his pleasure from his mother's stories and the little games she played with him. Now, twining his arms around Abhagi's neck and touching her cheek to his he got a shock.

'Why, Ma!' he exclaimed. 'You're burning with fever!' Then, with a tinge of anger in his voice, he added, 'Why did you have to stand in the sun all those hours? And bathe in the river on top of it? What's there to see in a burning corpse?'

'*Chhi*, Baba,' Abhagi scolded gently, putting her hand on his lips. 'You shouldn't use those words. They are sinful. It was not a burning corpse. It was our chaste and pure mistress, our revered Bamun Ma, going to heaven in a golden chariot.'

'What nonsense, Ma! As if people go to heaven in golden chariots!'

'I saw it with my own eyes, Kangali. She was sitting in the chariot. Her feet were crimson with alta. Everyone saw it.'

'Everyone saw it?'

'Everyone.'

Kangali leaned against his mother's breast, lost in thought. He believed his mother. He had been reared from infancy to have implicit faith in her. If she said she had seen this extraordinary spectacle and that others had seen it too, who was he to doubt her?

'Then,' he said, thoughtfully, 'you'll go to Heaven too. I heard Bindu's aunt saying to Rakhal's mother only the other day, "There's not another woman in our Duley clan as chaste and pure as Kangali's mother."'

Abhagi was silent.

'When Baba left you,' the boy continued slowly, hesitantly, 'so many people tried to persuade you to remarry. "No," you said, "why should I take another husband? I have my Kangali. He'll grow up and take care of me"' Then, his eyes filling up with tears, he added, 'What would have become of me, Ma, if you went away with another man? I would have starved to death.'

Abhagi put her arms around her son and pressed him to her bosom. '*Ma go!*' she murmured, thinking of those terrible days when the elders of the village were advising her, ceaselessly, to take another husband. But it wasn't only advice that had been showered on her. She had been pressured in so many different ways! She had been coaxed and cajoled, warned and threatened. Her ears had been filled with forebodings of her bleak future; of Kangali dying of starvation. But she hadn't been intimidated. She had clung to her resolve. Kangali saw the tears streaming down his mother's cheeks and felt his own eyes burn.

He twined his arms around her neck and asked tenderly, 'Do you want to lie down, Ma? Shall I make up a bed?'

Abhagi did not reply.

Kangali rolled out the mat and spread a kantha over it. Plucking a pillow from the machan, he smoothed it carefully. Then, taking his mother by the hand, he made her lie down. 'You needn't go back to work today,' Abhagi said to her son. 'Stay with me.'

The idea of skipping work and staying at home appealed to Kangali. But there was a hint of caution in his voice as he said, 'They won't give me the two paise for today if I...'

'Never mind.' Abhagi smiled. 'Come and lie down beside me. I'll tell you a story.'

Kangali needed no further invitation. Dropping down on the bed he curled his body against his mother's. 'Tell me the story of the rajputra and the kotalputra. And the flying horse,' he said, resting his cheek against hers.

Abhagi began her tale of the prince and the policeman's son and their adventures with the winged horse. It was an old fairy tale, heard over and over again during her childhood. But after a few minutes the two protagonists vanished from her story. As did the horse. She started weaving a web of fantasy that was entirely her own; something she hadn't heard from anyone at any time in her life. The higher her fever rose, the faster the hot blood pounded in her veins, the more impassioned the telling became and the more intricate her magic web of words. She spun tale after tale, without rest or respite, each more wonderful than the last. Kangali trembled with excitement and goose pimples broke out all over his slight frame. He pushed closer and closer to his mother's breast.

Slowly, the sun started dipping in the west. The falling shadows fell faster and pervaded the earth. Dusk crept into Abhagi's hut. But she did not rise to light the lamp or carry out the last duties of the day. Mother and son lay locked in an embrace, her voice crooning in his ears, sending shivers of thrill down his spine. It was the same story with variations, repeated over and over again. The story of the Brahmin lady's death – of the magnificent procession that had accompanied her to her last resting place, of the chariot in which she had sat on her way to Heaven. Of her weeping husband bidding her farewell after touching the dust of his feet to her brow, the fervent cries of *Bolo Hari, Hari Bol* as her sons lifted the bier on their manly shoulders. And then … then, the final triumph! Receiving her last fire from the hand of her eldest son…

'That fire was no ordinary fire, son,' Abhagi explained, her breath coming hotter and faster. 'It was Hari Himself! And the smoke rising up to the sky was not smoke. It was the chariot of heaven blazing a trail of glory. Kangalicharan! *Baba amaar!*' she cried out in an excess of emotion.

'Why, Ma?'

'If you light my pyre with your own hands, I'll go to Heaven too like Bamun Ma.'

Her words made Kangali uncomfortable. '*Jah!*' he said. 'You shouldn't say such things.'

But Abhagi went on as though she hadn't heard him. 'No one will look down upon me then. No one will shun me for my low birth. *Oof!*' Her face was flushed with excitement and her fevered breath came in gasps. 'Fire from my son's hand! Ah the glory of it! The chariot will have to come down for me. No one can stop it … for all that I am a poor untouchable…'

'Don't talk like that, Ma.' Kangali covered her mouth with his hand. 'It frightens me.'

'And, Kangali…' Abhagi pushed his hand gently away and continued on her own train of thought. 'Get hold of your father when my time comes and bring him here. Tell him he must give me the dust of his feet before I go. And … and my parting must be filled with sindoor and my feet lined with alta. But … but who will do all that for me? You will, won't you, Kangali? You are my son and my daughter. You are all I have.' Bursting into tears she kissed his cheek and laid her wet fevered face against his hair.

And now the drama of Abhagi's life was nearing curtain call. Only the final scene was left. There hadn't been much to the play. Her thirty years on the earth hadn't been remarkable in any way. And neither was her end.

Kaviraj Moshai, the only Ayurvedic practitioner in these parts, lived in another village. Kangali ran all the way, fell at his feet and begged him to come and see his mother. Met with a stony silence, he went back home, pawned the bell metal pitcher out of which they drank water and paid him his fee of one rupee. Still the great man did not deign to come. He handed Kangali a few pellets of medicine instead. Instructing him to grind them in a physician's pestle and mortar, mix the powder with ginger extract, honey and the juice of basil leaves, he told him to feed the potion to his mother in small doses.

Abhagi was amazed at what her son had done. 'Why did you pawn the pitcher without asking me, Baba?' she rebuked him gently. Then, taking the pellets from his hand she touched them to her forehead and threw them into the kitchen fire. 'If I'm fated to live, I'll do so anyway,' she said. 'Has anyone in our Bagdi Duley community ever taken a physician's medicine?'

Two or three days passed. Abhagi's neighbours heard of her illness and came to see her. They left without any offers of help. But each one knew of a remedy guaranteed to cure the ailing woman. 'Water in which a deer's horn has been soaked just can't fail,' one of them told Kangali. Another proposed burning cowrie shells and mixing the ash with honey. But the shells could not be ordinary ones. They had to be knuckled cowries. The mixture, fed to the patient, would bring instant relief.

Poor Kangali ran helter-skelter in search of these articles till Abhagi caught him by the hand and forced him to stop. 'If what the physician gave me was of no use, how can deer's horn and cowrie shells cure me? Give up running here and there and come and sit by me.'

'But you didn't take the pellets Kaviraj Moshai gave!' Kangali's face crumpled like that of a child. 'You threw them in the fire. How can you get well if you refuse everything?'

'I'll get well. Don't worry. Now wipe your eyes and listen to me. Put the pot on the hearth and boil some rice. Then sit by me and eat it. That will give me more comfort than any remedy in the world.'

Kangali rubbed his eyes with the edge of his dhuti and rose to obey his mother. For the first time in his life, he was cooking his own meal. But he could do nothing right. His fire wouldn't burn properly, his rice boiled down to a mush because he didn't know how to drain the starch and he spilt half of it when trying to transfer it to his kanshi. Abhagi watched him with an ache in her heart. Once, she even tried to rise from her bed, but her head swam and fell back on the pillow.

After the boy had gulped down some of the rice he had cooked, she called him to her side and tried to teach him how it had to be done. But her voice choked in her throat, and she couldn't speak.

Next morning Ishwar, the village barber, came to check Abhagi's pulse. He was good at this, and the villagers sent for him whenever anyone was seriously ill. Taking Abhagi's limp wrist between his fingers he frowned in thought. Then, sighing and shaking his head, he left the house. Abhagi understood what that meant. But the knowledge brought no fear. When everyone had gone, she whispered in Kangali's ear, 'Go to him now and bring him here. Tell him…'

'Who, Ma?'

'Your … you know who. He … the one who has moved to the other village.'

'Baba?'

Abhagi was silent. Kangali gazed on her face for a few moments and asked sadly, 'Why would he come here, Ma?'

'Tell him … tell him … that all I want is the dust of his feet. Nothing else.'

Kangali rose to go. Abhagi clutched his hand and said, 'Weep and plead a little, son. Tell him Ma is going…' Then, pausing for a few moments, she added, 'And on your way back, stop at the barber's house and ask his wife for a little alta. She is a kind woman and loves me. She will give it to you.'

Abhagi was only partially conscious when Rasik Bagh arrived the next morning. The shadow of death lay dark on her face. Her eyes seemed to have seen whatever there was to see in this world and were opening out to another ... a strange, uncharted, faraway world. Kangali wiped his cheeks and cleared his throat. 'Wake up, Ma,' he shook her gently by the arm, 'Baba is here. You wanted the dust of his feet'

Perhaps the mother heard. Perhaps she didn't. But the intense desire, hidden deep within her soul, shook her out of her somnolence. The dying woman moved her feeble arm to the edge of the bed and opened her palm. Rasik gazed at her with bewildered eyes. He hadn't, in his wildest imaginings, thought that the dust of his feet had any value; that anyone could desire it above all else in the world. He stood immobile with shock till Bindu's aunt, who stood by his side, prompted gently, 'Come, Baba. Give the poor girl a little dust from your feet.'

Rasik moved forward. His head teemed with thoughts and his chest felt tight with guilt. He had taken this woman as his wedded wife but had given her nothing. Not love, not protection, nor any means of sustenance. He had deprived her of everything that was her due without a thought. Yet she, even on her deathbed, wanted nothing from him but the dust of his feet. Rasik burst into tears.

'Such chastity and steadfastness are not to be seen even among Brahmin and Kayastha women,' Rakhal's mother exclaimed. 'Why she was born amongst us is beyond my understanding! But a task lies before you, Baba.' She turned her eyes on Rasik. 'You must arrange a cremation for her. Fire from Kangali's hand! She has yearned for it throughout her illness. It's almost as if death is nothing to her if only...'

The Creator who had chalked out the destiny of Abhagi, the ill-fated one, may or may not have heard the words. But they pierced young Kangali's heart with the sharpness of an arrow. The day passed and part of the night. Who knows if the chariot of heaven comes down to claim the souls of untouchables! Perhaps they are expected to hobble to their destinations, footsore and weary, in the darkness of night. Whatever be the truth, Abhagi did not wait for the dawn. She left the world before the sky had paled.

There was a wood apple tree growing outside Abhagi's hut. Borrowing an axe from one of the neighbours, Rasik proceeded to cut some branches from it. But before he could strike a single blow, the zamindar's guard came rushing to the scene. Landing a thundering slap on Rasik's cheek he yanked the axe from his hand. '*Saala*!' he shouted. 'How dare you touch this tree? Is it your father's property?'

Rasik rubbed his cheek ruefully without saying a word. But Kangali could not keep silent. 'My mother planted this tree with her own hands, Durwan-ji,' he protested. 'Why are you hitting Baba?'

Mouthing a string of abuses, the zamindar's retainer advanced aggressively. He raised a hand to strike Kangali, but dropped it. He had remembered just in time that the boy's mother had died, and he had, in all probability, touched the corpse.

His curses and threats had, in the meantime, brought some of the neighbours running to the scene. All of them admitted that it was wrong of Rasik to have cut the tree without taking the zamindar's permission. But they entreated Durwan-ji to use his kind offices and obtain the consent. It had been the dead woman's earnest desire, they told him, that her body be cremated. She had expressed this wish, over and over again, to everyone who had visited her during her illness. But all these pleas fell on deaf ears.

'Don't try these tricks with me.' The Bihari stalwart waved them away like flies. 'I know what I must do.'

*

The zamindar was not a local man and did not live in the village. But he kept a cutcherry here from which the business of the estate was conducted, and justice dispensed to the tenants. But being an absentee landlord, all magisterial power and responsibility had been vested in the person of the steward, Adhar Rai. Now, while the neighbours were still begging and pleading with the durwan, Kangali ran, not stopping for breath, all the way to the cutcherry. He had heard that the lesser minions of the estate were corrupt and expected bribes for everything they did. But if the story of this gross injustice reached the zamindar's ears, redress would surely follow, he reasoned. But alas! Young and inexperienced, Kangali hadn't a clue to the true nature of the Bengali zamindar and his appointed officials. Trembling with grief and anxiety, the newly bereaved, motherless boy dashed up the steps and stood before the lord and master of the cutcherry.

Adhar Rai had just concluded his morning prayers and eaten a light breakfast in preparation for the day. Coming out on the veranda he was shocked and angered to see the apparition before him.

'*Ke re*?' he thundered. 'Who are you?'

'I'm Kangali. Durwan-ji has beaten my father.'

'Rightly served. He must have defaulted on the rent.'

'No, Babu Moshai. My mother died last night, and my father was cutting the tree in front of our house when…' Unable to go on Kangali burst into tears.

At this, Adhar Rai lost his temper. 'What are you doing here if your mother's dead?' he snapped. 'Get off those steps and stand in the yard.' Inwardly he shivered with alarm. The boy must have touched the corpse before coming to the cutcherry. Who knew if he had touched anything here?

'*Orey!*' he called out to a servant. 'Bring a pot of cow-dung water and sprinkle it on the steps and veranda. The whole place is polluted.' Then, turning to Kangali, he asked, 'What caste are you?'

Thoroughly frightened by now Kangali ran down the steps and answered meekly, 'We are Duley, Babu Moshai.'

'A Duley's corpse,' Adhar Rai muttered thoughtfully. 'Where's the need for wood then?'

'My mother wanted a cremation. "You must light my pyre with your own hands," she said to me over and over again. All the neighbours know. Why don't you ask them, Babu Moshai? Everyone heard her…'

'If you want to cremate your mother, you must leave five rupees in the cutcherry. That's the price of the tree. Can you do it?'

Kangali knew he couldn't. He had pawned the last vessel in the house, the kanshi from which he ate his rice, for one rupee, to buy his mourning scarf. He shook his head.

'No, Babu,' he said, softly.

Adhar Rai bared his teeth in a grimace. 'Then go bury the corpse on the bank of the river as befits your caste. How dare your father raise an axe to the zamindar's tree? Is it his father's property? Good-for-nothing wretch! Rogue! Scoundrel!'

'But the tree grows in our yard, Babu Moshai. My mother planted it with her own hands.'

'*Hunh!* Planted it with her own hands ... Pandey!' Adhar Rai called out to the guard. 'Take the boy by the scruff of his neck and throw him out of the cutcherry.'

Pandey, in the manner of all faithful retainers, acted even before the words had left his master's lips. Giving the boy a hard shove, he threw him to the ground, mouthing a stream of curses for good measure. Kangali stood up, shook the dust from his dhuti and walked slowly away. His eyes were dazed. What had he done to deserve such treatment? He hadn't a clue.

Adhar Rai saw the expression on the boy's face, but it didn't make a dent in his conscience. He was made of sterner stuff. Dusting his hands as at a job well done, he called out to the clerk. 'Paresh! Find out if the father has defaulted on the rent. If so, go to his house and confiscate his household goods. Brass vessels, fishing nets ... whatever you find. The bastard might try to escape.'

*

There were just two days left for the sraddha. Old Mukhopadhyay Moshai was busy supervising the arrangements. His wife's last rites were to be conducted with all the pomp and fanfare owing to her as a rich man's wife and the mother of many sons. There was a lot of work to be done.

'Thakur Moshai!' Kangali came and stood before him. 'My mother's dead.'

'Who are you?' The old man's brow furrowed, 'What do you want?'

'I'm Kangali. My mother asked me to cremate her.'

'Then go ahead and do it.'

Kangali stood silent not knowing what to say. The story of his treatment at the cutcherry had made the rounds, in the meantime, and many of the villagers were aware of it. 'I think he wants a tree,' one of the men standing by ventured to explain, following it up with details of the boy's encounter with Adhar Rai.

'What audacity!' Mukhopadhyay Moshai cried out in shock. 'Wants a tree indeed! That too at a time when I need all the wood I can find for my own event! Just two days are left for the sradhha. I'm neck deep in my own troubles and the brat sails in demanding a tree. *Jah! Jah!* You'll get nothing here. Try your luck elsewhere.'

The old man walked away with a furious clacking of wooden clogs.

Bhattacharya Moshai, the family priest, was sitting a little distance away making lists of the articles he would need for the last rites. Looking up at the boy he said, 'The right of cremation has not been ordained for your caste. All you need to do is set alight a twist of dry grass, touch the flame to the mouth of the corpse and then bury it on a bank of the river.'

In the middle of this scene, Mukhopadhyay Moshai's eldest son walked in. He had been allotted several tasks by his father and he was rushing about seeing to them. He heard the priest's ruling and observed caustically, 'Do you see, Bhattacharya Moshai? How low-born buggers want to ape the upper castes these days? Such are the times we live in.' He hastened out of the room without waiting for an answer.

Kangali stood silent for a while. The last two-and-a-half hours had turned him from an eager, trusting child to an adult. A wise, wary, discerning adult. Head bowed, he walked away, came home and sat by his dead mother.

Now the men and women of the community took over. A pit was dug on the left bank of the Garud and Abhagi's body lowered into it. Rakhal's mother took a knot of burning straw and put it in Kangali's hand. Then, taking it in hers, she guided the flame towards the mouth of the corpse. That done, the straw was thrown away and earth piled on her till every trace of Abhagi was obliterated.

The men sweated and toiled shovelling earth into his mother's grave, but Kangali had no eyes for them. He stood at a little distance, his gaze fixed on the thrown away knot of straw. The flame had died down, but a tiny wisp of smoke still rose from it. Up and up, it went … a faint thin wisp of bluish smoke. Kangali stared at it with eyes that had turned to stone.

The Insect Festival

Anil Ghorai

Larani's jaws were so wide and her open mouth so large, the neighbours said she looked like a she-devil and had nicknamed her Rakshashi. Another of her flaws was a high forehead which rose like a dome right up to her hairline. Her old mother criticized her for these imperfections incessantly and showered her with advice. 'Larani re!' she would say, 'a face like yours is cursed. Only evil can come out of such a mouth. That's why I keep telling you, again and again, to think ten times before opening it. And stop gadding about in the neighbourhood. Stay quietly at home and help me with the housework. When a woman's body swells and ripens with the sap of youth she must keep it within bounds. If she runs from door to door, like a restless otter between water and land, she will fall on a stony bank and break all her bones.'

But Larani wouldn't listen to a word. Baring bright red gums and large protruding teeth, she laughed away her mother's advice. Her mouth opened as wide as the boy Krishna's when his mother Jashoda looked into it and saw a whole cosmos within … innumerable spheres spinning in harmony.

'Cover your mouth,' the old woman would shriek in disgust, 'and stop this demoniac laughter. Mother Earth will shudder on hearing it and her surface will crack with fear. Living trees will turn to deadwood.'

Larani was her only child but not a drop of sympathy for her moistened the mother's dry shrivelled breast. And ...why should it? Larani was a burden on her. She was as unlike other girls as possible and rearing her was agony. She pranced about the village, her heavy breasts swaying shamelessly, climbed trees exposing her legs and thighs and dived into the village pond whenever she felt like it. She swam for hours, whole afternoons together. And she was so greedy, she didn't hesitate a second before setting off on a walk to eat bhog at a Vaishnav festival in a village three miles away.

The old woman's hut was one of the dozen or so in Harhi Parha. Harhis belonged to the tanner caste and were constrained to live in a neighbourhood of their own as far away from the dwellings of the upper castes as possible. Hola Burho's hut, which was also his *khol ghar* or workroom, was situated at the extreme edge of the parha. He was fifty years old, so thin and frail that he looked like a cadaver. He made a living by repairing drums. His son Pabna went by the nickname of Tagan Master. Why *Tagan Master*? It had been given in jest by the neighbours. The swiftness and skill with which he could skin an animal had earned him the name. The neighbours laughed at him but admired him all the same.

Pabna was a sweeper in the government hospital of the adjoining town and lived in the quarters allotted to him. He was a fine drummer and was often invited to perform at the festivals held in and around the town. He earned good money but didn't give his father a paisa or offer to help him with his work. The old man suffered incessantly from poverty and want.

Pabna was of no use to Hola Burho but Larani made up for Pabna's filial neglect. She called the old man Khurho, uncle, and spent nearly the whole day in his service. She prepared his hookah, fetched water from the pond and made *gaab*, the concoction he needed to baste his drums. The chief ingredient for it was worm-eaten earth which wasn't easily accessible. It would have been impossible for the decrepit old man to scour the village paths looking for earthworm mounds and, if it hadn't been for Larani, he would have had to give up his occupation.

Larani loved spending time with the old man and watching his gnarled old hands as they moved lovingly over the drums, layering the base with gaab, stretching the leather and tightening the strings.

Hola Burho's hut was fairly large. It had two rooms with a thatched roof and earthen walls rising seven feet from the ground. It had several windows through which breeze surged with a rushing sound and light came streaming in. Behind it was a paddy field and half a mile away was the infamous Danga Porhiyar Maath where Larani's father had been cremated, years ago, by the village folk. To the right of Hola Burho's hut was a banana clump and, swirling at its roots, lay a stretch of water as deep as a length of bamboo. When the rains failed and other people's ponds turned to dust, Hola Burho's was alive with fish. Silvery cheetal darted over the surface and katla, with scales as big as rupee coins, somersaulted in the muddy water. Larani watched them with wonder-filled eyes.

'What are you staring at, little one?' the old man would call out to her affectionately. 'Come, sit by me. I'll tell you the story of the great storm that raged in these parts in the year … now what was the year? Ah yes. It was forty-nine. Now listen carefully…'

'Yes, yes, Khurho.' Larani would creep close to the old man, the pupils dancing in her tiny eyes. Then, seeing him absorbed in his work and taking his time, she would cry out impatiently, 'Tell. Tell na…'

'Su-u-ch a storm … su-u-ch a storm,' the old man would begin his oft-told tale in a leisurely fashion, dragging out the words, pausing for effect every now and then, 'as was ne-v-er seen in this village or in a-a-ny other for that matter…' He would go back to his drum till Larani gave him a push. 'What was I saying?' he would take up his story once again. 'Ah yes. The storm. The water in this hut rose to the thatch and the current … ah! the current … it pulled at people's feet and tore them away from the ground. First there was the wind. Then waves of salt water entered the village with such force that…'

His voice would trail away and he would peer at his drum till Larani gave him another push. 'No one had seen anything like it,' he would take a deep breath and go on. 'The walls of our huts melted into the water like sandesh. Giant bamboos crashed to the ground. Cows and goats were swept away…'

'Why, Khurho?' Larani's eyes gleamed with fearful glee. 'What caused such a terrible storm? And, storm or no storm, where did the *salt* water come from?'

'That's a long story. To hear it would make your flesh creep. Your hair will stand on end. Human beings commit sins and suffer for them. Sometimes from their own; sometimes from those of others.' He paused, lifted his dhuti, and scratched the scaly skin of his thigh. 'So, what was I saying? Ah! Yes. Sin. There was a widow living somewhere in these parts. A loose woman named Taramoni. She got pregnant and delivered a dead foetus. Now where was she to hide it? Not knowing what to do, she threw the bloody clot into the sea. Sea Mother was horrified at her waters being polluted by the fruit of fornicating mortals and vowed revenge. She first started simmering with rage, then boiled over. Angry waves rose sky high and flooded all the houses in the surrounding villages. Could any mortal stop her fury? Arre ... na ... na. Whose chest is so broad and strong that it can stand against a vengeful sea?'

Hola Burho had a good stock of tall tales like this one. He had witnessed many strange incidents in his life and had kept them tucked away in his head. He came up with one or two, occasionally, and served them up in a duly embellished and exaggerated form. And in Larani's presence they poured out, like water from a hosepipe, from his withered old mouth.

Larani was a quick sprightly girl, not given to sitting in one place and listening patiently to anyone. But she loved Hola Burho's stories. As she heard his tale of the loose widow Taramoni, and how she was responsible for the destruction of an entire village, she felt her heart sink with dread. The old man's ash-grey eyes, dimmed with age like an ancient cat's, held hers like a magnet. Her body stiffened like a blighted palm.

'*Hahn re,* Larani.' Her mother accosted her from time to time. 'What do you see in that piece of carrion? What evil mantra does he hiss in your ear that makes you stick by his side all day long? He's not a good man. He had a glad eye for women in his youth. Heed my warning. Don't go near his hut again. He may be old and decrepit now but a snake has poison in its jaws even after its fangs have fallen out. Stay at home and strip palm leaves with me. The sticks make fine brooms. When we've made a dozen or so, I'll go sell them at the weekly haat. The work will stop you from gadding about the village and bring some money in as well.'

Poverty and hardship had clung, like cobwebs, in the lives of mother and daughter for as long as Larani could remember. Things got so bad during the rainy season that their rice pot saw fire only once in a while. But now the rains were over and the skies trembled with a soft blue sheen. In the long rays of a golden sun a few clumps of kash could be seen by the riverbank, their feathery brooms swaying in the breeze. Emerald meadows tossed their limbs in a voluptuous dance. Autumn sap ran through paddy stalks swelling their virgin breasts. On the furrows, green with moss, black-and-white crabs crept fearfully before slipping into their holes.

Larani stood on one of them and gazed into the distance with wistful eyes. At the road over which the bus had taken Pabna to the city that day. Pabna had left at dawn without a word to her. Pain gnawed at her breast. Her eyes burned with unshed tears. She couldn't keep her lips from trembling. Had she offended him in some way? But what had she done? She couldn't think of anything. If only he had stopped by and told her what it was, she would have begged for forgiveness. Her best friend had told her that men who went to the city to make a living forgot their past. They had no feelings left for their village and the people in it. Did that mean Pabna had changed? That she meant nothing to him anymore. That, like a chameleon, he had taken on another colour? A sharp needle pierced her heart at the thought.

It was the month of ashwin. Soon the drums would begin to roll, heralding the coming of Uma. What a beautiful season this was! The sky so blue; the earth such a vivid green. So many wild, sweet odours wafting in the breeze. One was her own woman scent. A fragrance rising from her young limbs mixed with that of baked earth which clung to them all the time. Pabna had said he loved her scent. But would he be able to catch it from so far away? She thought not.

'*A ha ha*!' Pabna would exclaim in admiration every time she gave him the gaab she had prepared. 'You've worked a miracle. A layer of this at the base of any drum will make the leather leap up with joy. The deepest, most vibrant sounds will come from it. There's magic in your hands, Larani. I feel like clasping them in my own and kissing them.' Such were the things Pabna had said to her back then. Words so beautiful, they sent a shiver down her spine. Her limbs shuddered in ecstasy. What had happened? Why had he gone silent now?

Larani's heart felt as though it would break under its own weight. Her eyes streamed silently as she walked the village paths looking for worm mounds. She longed to share her misery with someone; to hear a few words of consolation. But she knew it would do no good. Her sorrow, which she kept hidden in the innermost depths of her being, would travel from one ear to a dozen ears and turn into a subject of gossip. Her agony would increase tenfold...

'There's no need to go to the old man's hut today,' her mother had said to her only that morning. 'Does he give you a paisa for the work he makes you do? Go, cut some fronds from the date palms at the edge of the village. Just a couple of bundles will do. It's a nice bright day and the air is crisp and hot. The fronds will dry in no time. We should be able to make enough brooms to sell at the haat and buy salt and oil with the money.'

But Larani had turned a deaf ear to the old woman's advice. The drum repairer's workshop drew her like a magnet. She was aware of a strange peace, the kind she felt when offering prayers at the Sheetala temple, all the time that she was there. It wasn't that she didn't think of Pabna. She did. But the work occupied her thoughts even more often.

Hola Burho had many customers. In their own village and in several others surrounding it. Among them were kirtaniyas and other Vaishnavs. Followers of the Mahaprabhu, they wore saffron, bore the marks of their sect in sandalwood paste on their brows and, frenzied with Krishna love, sang songs of the dalliance of Radha and Krishna, accompanied with drums and cymbals. They had to keep their drums functional at all times. In consequence they were constrained to run to Hola Burho's hut every other day.

Hola Burho's wife was old and frail. Her eyes were ridden with cataracts, thick as fish scales, and she was almost blind. It was Larani who had to roll out mats for these respected customers to sit on, serve paan and water and light hookahs for them. But even more demanding than these jobs was preparing the gaab for Hola Burho's drums. It was a lot of work. She had to walk through the village, eyes skinned, looking for worm pats. These had to be collected, baked in the kiln and crushed into a fine dust. But even that was not enough. The dust had to be passed through a thin cloth to render it finer, then mixed with fermented rice to create a smooth sticky paste.

The work is far more difficult than it sounds. And a special skill is needed. Hola Burho had taken pains to teach her the art. But after she had mastered it, he had left the making of gaab completely to her. So, if Larani didn't turn up one day, or left the hut in a huff, he had to pick up his stick, go tottering to her mother's house and beg her to return…

That afternoon as she was walking back from the lake, the worm pats she had gathered tied in her anchal, her friend Menaka accosted her. 'Come,' Menaka whispered urgently, a tentative smile fading from her lips. Taking Larani by the hand she drew her away from the path to the edge of a paddy field. 'Listen,' she said, 'I need to talk to you. Have you heard the news?'

'No, I haven't heard anything.'

Menaka's face turned grim with disbelief. She glared at Larani. The pupils of her eyes popped open, as big and round as kul berries. 'I don't believe it,' she said angrily. 'How can you not have heard…?' Then, seeing the innocence and surprise on Larani's face, she continued. 'Insects are coming in from the west. They will reach the village any day now and devour the paddy crop. There will be no harvest for us this year.'

'*Dur*!' Larani laughed away Menaka's fears. 'How you exaggerate! Insects come every year. But they don't eat the entire crop. Look around you. The stalks are so heavy with grain, every granary in the village will brim over.'

'I hope you are right.' Menaka turned her face towards the temple of Goddess Sheetala, folded her hands and touched them to her brow. Then, in a voice moist and heavy with tears, she continued, 'Baba has promised to wed me in agrahayan if the paddy crop is good. With the boy from Paniparul. I told you about him, didn't I? He has seen me and likes me. I like him too. He has a government job in the city and makes a good living. I am sick and tired of being a spinster, Larani. And of being stuck in this village. I'm dying to escape.'

Larani didn't pay much heed to what Menaka said to her. Insects inhabited the land just as humans did. If one dragged a net through a pond, insects got trapped in it along with fishes. And even if a good many came flying through the air … it wasn't the end. They rested for a while in the fields, nibbled at a bit of grain, then flew away. Besides, there were ways of getting rid of them. So many different kinds of pesticides were available at the shops in town. Larani knew some of the names … not all.

Larani stood where she was for a while after Menaka left. She took a deep, deep breath. The scent of the earth she carried in her anchal, mingling with the remembered one of Pabna's sweat-soaked limbs, rose like a cloud in the air and suffused her senses. *A ha ha* … the sweetest fragrance on earth. Larani's eyes closed in ecstasy.

Larani looked up at the sky. She remembered another time. A time when fields heavy with paddy had indeed been reduced to stubble. It wasn't insects who had wreaked the havoc. It was drought. A terrible, unprecedented drought had swept through the land, scorching and burning the waving green; turning it to dust and ashes. That was the time Larani had become aware of her new womanhood. A hitherto unknown emotion was creeping into her heart, softly and secretly, opening it like a lotus bud. Her cheeks were flushed; her eyes downcast as she followed Pabna to the mahotsav in Bamun Parha two miles away.

Twilight had given way to dusk by the time they walked back. The fields on either side of the path were dark with falling night. Gusts of hot wind stung her limbs like the fangs of a snake. A noxious smell of burning rubber filled her nostrils. It came from the flaming cycle tyre Pabna held in his hands. Her stomach felt tight and heavy with the bhog she had eaten. Coarse rice, cheap biruli dal and pumpkin curry. Pabna had held her hand that day. 'Hanh re,' he had asked tenderly, 'have you eaten your fill? Tell me if you are still hungry. I've brought back some bhog tied in my gamchha. I'll give it to you.'

Larani feels her heart quake whenever she remembers those words. Her limbs shiver as though with a high fever. But soon afterwards another feeling suffuses her; a sweet warmth like the scent of baked earth. Dreams fill her eyes. Dreams of a tiny nest with only Pabna and she in it. Then her face takes on the shine of freshly mixed gaab. Her lips break into a smile, joyous as the beat of a drum…

⋆

Five drums lay side by side in Hola Burho's khol ghar, waiting to be repaired. All that he needed to do to them was scrape the old gaab away, apply fresh coats, then put them out in the sun to dry. When the new gaab turned crackling crisp, he would stretch the leather and tighten the strings. Money had been scarce during the rainy season with hardly any work. The amount the repair of the drums brought him would come in useful.

But the weather was playing tricks. Hola Burho peered at the sky anxiously. Though it was the month of ashwin, columns of cloud had been rising from the east since morning. Rain would start falling any moment now and with the rain swarms of insects would come swooping down. The work of drum repairing was very difficult when it rained. The earth for the gaab softened and turned moist minutes after it had left the kiln. Grinding and straining it was well-nigh impossible.

Larani had been struggling with her baked earth since morning. 'Go, child,' the old man said to her, 'tell your Khurhi Ma to give you some leftover rice. Eat your fill. How will you work on an empty stomach? Preparing gaab isn't child's play. One can't be lax and casual with it. If the mixture isn't perfect, the drum is angry. Instead of emitting a deep, sweet sound it growls when it is touched.'

'You're right, Khurho,' Larani turned her head and smiled at the old man. 'Patience is the main thing in khol repairing. Drums are sensitive. They protest if the repairer is clumsy or in a hurry.'

'Absolutely! Absolutely!' Hola Burho slapped his thigh in hearty agreement. 'You've hit the nail on the head. You have a lot of patience, Larani. You are the right person for the job. My worthless son thinks he has become a nawab. Too high and mighty for drum repairing. My business will come to an end the day I close my eyes.'

'I won't let that happen, Khurho.'

'Will you be able to keep it going?' The old man paused for a moment and muttered worriedly, 'The age of kirtan is coming to an end. Drums and cymbals are collecting dust. No one calls for kirtan parties anymore. No ... not even for a funeral procession. The young are only interested in hearing English bands.'

Hola Burho's old white head shook from side to side with worry. His wrinkled face turned as slack as the sagging leather of a discarded drum. A shuddering breath rose from his hollowed ribcage. His tiny eyes, dimmed with age, were fixed on Larani's face. It gleamed as though coated in sweat and gurjan oil, like that of Goddess Durga. The unattractive face with its wide mouth and high forehead was transformed. It had acquired the shy sweetness of a land lotus.

'Why are you staring at me, Khurho?' Larani asked, surprised. 'Look around you. There's so much work to be done. This is no time to get lost in your thoughts. If we don't hurry, we won't be able to deliver the drums in time.'

'Yes, yes, of course.' The old man pulled himself together. 'You're right, Larani. I don't know why but I feel very weak and spent these days. It has been so ever since the boy left home and started living in the city. My spirit is broken. All my strength and resolution have left me.'

'You must persuade him to return. Why should he work for strangers when his father has such a flourishing khol repair business? If he handles it properly, he won't need to worry about money ever again.'

The words left Larani's lips before she could stop them. But they weren't only words. They were a mantra she kept hidden deep within her and chanted silently, every moment of her waking hours. Today they had fallen, like autumn leaves, before the old man. She turned red with shame. Inadvertently, she had laid bare her soul. She felt stripped of all cover like a tree with stark branches.

But Hola Burho didn't seem to notice her dismay. He picked up the pestle and started tapping it on the wooden frame of one of the drums. Then, with quick flicks of his fingers on the leather, he tested the sound. He kept working at the wooden base, leather and strings till he heard the sound he wanted to hear. Finally, with a sigh of satisfaction, he leaned back and said, 'Sing a song, Larani. You know the one I like to hear.'

'Khurhi Ma will scold me.' Larani hesitated a little. 'Let's get on with our work for now. I'll come over this evening and sing it.'

Even as she spoke, a customer appeared at the door of the khol ghar. Larani rose to her feet and unrolled a mat, then hastened inside to fetch water and a hookah. Hola Burho shook off his lethargy. 'Take a seat, Madhav Babu,' he said hospitably. 'Make yourself comfortable.'

'The girl is very attached to you, I see.' Madhav Boshtom smiled. 'Every time I come to your khol ghar I see her doing some work or other. She has no father … so I've heard. Why don't you wed her to your Pabna? They will make a first-class pair! They'll fit together like a pot and a lid.'

Hola Burho started coughing. He coughed incessantly till it seemed as though all the breath would leave his lungs. His eyes filled with painful tears. Wiping them away with the back of his hand he gasped, 'You have taken the words out of my mouth, Madhav Babu. I love the girl more than her true father did. Nothing would give me more satisfaction than to see her as my daughter-in-law. Beauty is not everything. Virtue and character are more important in a woman. And, in these two, she has no peer. She is so industrious … she can take on the work of ten men and carry it out to perfection. As for her skill at khol repair work, sometimes I feel she is even better than me. The gaab she makes is flawless. Fit for the drums of heaven.'

'Then get the wedding over and done with. *Shubhashya shighram*. The shastras advise swift action in a good cause. Why delay it?'

'It's my son. He has left the village and gone to live in the city.'

'Doesn't he come home?'

'Only once in a while. He used to come quite often earlier. But now he has to be coaxed and cajoled. I wonder what has gone wrong. He's my only son. I spend sleepless nights worrying about him.'

'Hari! Hari!' Madhav Boshtom suppressed a yawn. 'Once a lad breathes city air, he loses his love for his native village. I can't say I blame your son. Our village has gone to the dogs. We could buy pure ghee once. Can we do so now? Everything is adulterated. We were a peaceful community at one time. But now all we have left is infighting and ganging up on one another.'

At this point seven other customers walked in with drums wrapped in white cloth. One of them had the sectarian marks of the Vaishnav etched all over his body. His feet were bare and his eyes had the glazed look of a true devotee. They settled down on the mat, took out bidis from their pockets and lit them. 'Hola-da,' one of them said between puffs, 'we've brought our drums for repair. They are in bad shape. The leather is covered in mildew. They've been lying useless throughout the rainy season. But now that we hear Ma Durga's footsteps, things might improve. That's why we've come rushing to you.'

'Times are bad in other ways too,' a man called Kanu Hazra said in a solemn voice. 'The gods are angry. We need to hold a kirtan in the village to propitiate them.'

'Why? What has happened?'

'Insects have ruined my paddy crop. Three bighas of ripening grain destroyed. A stone, the size of a mountain, is weighing down my chest. The gods have turned against me. I feel lost … devastated.'

Kanu Hazra used to be a drum player at one time. But now he ran a business in the city. He repaired radios and sold audiocassettes and microphones. Hindi songs blared from his shop all day long. Hola Burho was startled at the utter despair in the man's voice. Not knowing how to respond, he began blabbering about the time the fish in the village ponds had caught a terrible skin affliction. Not one was spared. Some lost their tails, some their fins and scales. Others had heads covered with sores. To look at them was to feel nauseated. The villagers were in a state of shock. Many had given up eating fish for months afterwards…

Hola Burho had thought, at first, that the disease was caused by pollution. Some ponds had been left unclean for many years and their water had become infected. The germs had spread to the rest of the waterbodies in the village. Some others said that what they were witnessing was a fish cancer. But Larani had an interesting view. 'Na … na, Khurho,' she had said solemnly. 'This is a scourge that has come from Heaven. Fish are like men. They attack and feed on one another. Can they go unpunished?'

Hola Burho gathered his working materials; needle, twine, gaab, pestle and mortar. Then drawing a half-smoked bidi from behind his ear, he lit it and took a deep puff. His chest swelled with self-importance. Blowing a cloud of smoke in the air, he looked around the room. So many distinguished men of the village were here, sitting on the floor of his khol ghar. Why? Because they were in trouble and needed him. He was the best khol repairer in these parts. And as such he, why only he, even his forefathers commanded respect. He had brought glory to his family. He felt his soul expand, grow rich. The triumph a gecko feels when it has a fly trapped in its gummy mouth swept over him. His eyes held the same expression as he looked on the faces of his customers. They were like insects before him. Fluttering helplessly, waiting on his mercy.

These people were rich. They owned paddy fields and lived in brick houses. Yet they were sitting in his hut, today, with long worried faces. Hola Burho had nothing at all except his skill. An invaluable skill. It would enable him to squeeze a good deal of money out of these desperate men. He smiled snidely to himself and said, 'Yes, yes. Times are hard indeed. This insect menace is hurting every business. Drum repairing is getting tougher and tougher every day. Who knows but I might be forced to wind it up.'

The alarm on the faces before him sent a thrill down his spine and he added, 'The price of every item has jumped twofold. One has to pay through one's nose for the smallest bit of cow skin. Goat skin is cheaper but can't be used for drums. Why … even simple things like earth, paint, stone chips and gaab have become unaffordable. What do I do? My customers snap at me if I ask them to pay a little more. But I am at my wit's end. I beg them with folded hands to find another drum repairer. But no. They have to come to me.'

The men glanced at one another. Their eyes were wary. They hadn't realized that the wily old man was conning them. A long silence followed. It was broken by Madhav Boshtom. Scratching noisily at a patch of ringworm near his crotch he said, 'I heard about the insect menace from Poob Parha. Everyone I met is paralysed with fear. Someone in the village must have committed some grievous sin. That is why we are being tested like this.'

'Don't talk nonsense, Madhav,' the elderly Brajalal admonished. 'Insects haven't appeared only in our village. The whole country is afflicted by them. I heard over the radio, last evening, that scientists are advising farmers to spray their fields with pesticide. But it isn't working. More and more are coming in from Heaven knows where. We are facing a very serious problem. If they devour all the grain, the price of rice will go sky high. People will die of starvation.'

Kanai Maiti, unlike Hola Burho's other customers, was a man of some education. He even had a degree from the college in Kanthi. He read newspapers and gave his opinion on every subject as though he had all the knowledge of the world at his fingertips. 'Listen,' he pronounced in a commanding voice, 'pay full attention to what I'm saying. Have you heard of the war against Saddam Hussain? Do you have *any* idea of how many bombs were exploded? Won't the earth react? The oxygen in the air is severely depleted. In consequence insects have proliferated. We all know that insects thrive in filthy, polluted areas. The trouble is that, today, the entire earth is polluted. It has become a breeding ground for all manner of pests.'

Many among his audience hadn't a clue to what Kanai was saying. Yet they listened to him with reverence. He was a man of learning. His words couldn't be dumped in the ash pit.

Hola Burho neither understood nor cared to understand Kanai Maiti's words of wisdom. Dismissing him completely he came back to his earlier point. 'Listen, *babu sakal*,' he turned to the others. 'Circumstances have changed ... we are all agreed on that. You have come to me with your drums. Now please tell me what I need to do. You are all busy and important men. I don't wish to keep you waiting...' His knees danced with impatience.

Brajalal rose to his feet. Going to the door, he spat a stream of betel juice on the ground and resumed his seat. Wiping his mouth with the palm of his hand he pronounced in a solemn voice. 'We've come to you because we are facing a crisis. There's a saying, I'm sure you've heard it, that a man dying of thirst will drink even the foul water of a stagnant pond.' A minute of silence followed. Then, wagging his head at the others as though seeking approval, he continued, 'A meeting was held in the village yesterday. It was decided that pesticide will be sprayed in every nook and corner of each parha. Apart from that, kirtan parties will sing *naam gaan*, the name of God, every Thursday and Saturday. A procession of singers will emerge from the Sheetala temple and go all around the village. Right up to the edge, stopping only at the wooden bridge near the cremation ground. Drums, in good shape, will be required to accompany the singing. So, as you see, Hola da, we've brought you seven drums. You will have to repair them quickly. Let us see if these methods work. If the Gods relent and save us from this insect menace…'

Kanai Maiti had been listening to Brajalal all this while with a scowl on his face. Now he burst into speech. Hissing like a tomcat he cried, 'You're talking nonsense, Brajalal babu. A cow dies if you pour poison down his throat; not if you mix it in its dung. This is the age of science. Instead of singing kirtan, what we should be doing is spraying the crops with a high dose of pesticide.'

Brajalal's ego suffered a terrible blow at these words. He turned on Kanai Maiti with all the disdain he was capable of. 'What do you know of the power of naam gaan? You … a boy of yesterday! Just because you can read a few pages of English, you think you know everything?' The others, making a complete U-turn, nodded in agreement. The cornered Kanai Maiti fell silent.

'The decision taken by the elders in the meeting is final,' Brajalal continued with a triumphant glance at the now subdued

Kanai. 'We must follow it to the letter.' Taking a bidi out of his pocket he lit it, took a few puffs and continued ponderously, 'It has also been decided that everyone in the village should turn vegetarian for the next two months. Forget eating ... we mustn't even touch fish, meat and eggs. Getting rid of pests sent by Heaven to test us mortals is no joke. A great deal of sacrifice is necessary. We will call upon the gods, of course. We will beg for their help through yagnas and prayers. But these must be accompanied with abstinence and renunciation on everyone's part. Men, women and children ... all. Only then will the scourge be contained. Otherwise, even the great Lord Krishna will not be able to save us.'

Hola Burho's white head swayed in agreement. 'The idea is a good one, Brajalal babu,' he said. 'Yagnas and kirtan unaccompanied by self-control and self-denial will seem as though we are celebrating a festival. We should be prepared to fast, too, if necessary.'

'Well said.' Brajalal rose to his feet. 'You are a man of experience and know the difference between right and wrong.' The others rose too. 'We'll come back after three days,' Brajalal added with a satisfied grin. 'Please keep the drums ready.'

*

Seven or eight days later...

It was high noon, with the sun at its zenith. The sky was a scintillating blue with not a speck of cloud to dim its clarity. There was no breeze either. The air was so hot and still, it seemed as though all the winds of the earth had been driven away to another planet. Not a leaf stirred. Larani met Menaka at the mouth of the narrow lane that led to Harhi Parha. Menaka was dressed in her best sari and held a brass plate filled with pieces of fruit and sweets in her hands. Her face streamed with sweat. She was returning from the Sheetala temple after offering prayers.

Menaka had been having sleepless nights of late. Anxiety was gnawing at her heart with sharp teeth. A terrible restlessness had taken hold of her. The insect menace was showing no sign of receding. The paddy stalks that had been so thick, green and luscious until a few weeks ago, now looked like the rickety legs of a diseased child. 'It seems as though the paddy crop will fail this year too,' her father had said to her only this morning. 'I thought I'd be able to get rid of you after the harvest, but I'll have to put off the wedding till the next. What can I do? The gods are against me. They don't know how it feels to have a great girl like you sitting on my chest. I feel choked. As though a demon is squeezing all the air out of my lungs.'

Heart-wrenching words. Menaka ran out of the room weeping bitterly. Sobbing her heart out, she made a resolution. She would take matters in her own hands. She would find a husband for herself. If she kept waiting for her father to arrange a marriage the *old maid* stigma would never leave her...

Larani knew that Menaka had been dying to get married for years. She felt sorry for her but never brought up the subject. She had enough troubles of her own. What comfort could she give her friend when she, herself, was in the same boat? Menaka wiped her face with her anchal and put a piece of cucumber and half a sandesh in Larani's hand. 'I went to the fields last evening, Larani. The insects...' She couldn't go on. Looking at her pale, worn face and trembling lips, it seemed to Larani that the insects hadn't just devoured the paddy. They had nibbled their way into Menaka's heart and turned it into a sieve with a thousand holes. She folded her hands in reverence to the goddess, put the prasad in her mouth and said, 'How much power do insects have against the strength and brains of men? How long can they go on fighting us? They will have to succumb in the end. Just wait a few more days. They will take wing and fly away to other lands before long.'

'But they will devastate the fields before they go.' Menaka looked at Larani with lacklustre eyes. 'Our problem is that we have no unity. The wise and experienced elders of the village had discussed the matter and decided that, to propitiate the gods, everyone was to give up eating meat and fish. But was the decision followed? On the very next evening, Subal Dom's wife roasted a sukoi fish and ate it. What kind of unholy behaviour is this? How can we escape the menace if everyone doesn't cooperate? The crops will be destroyed, Larani. Not a trace will be left.'

'I don't agree. The poor woman is pregnant. She craved some roasted fish and ate it. Why should that bring harm to the whole village? I don't see any connection between eating fish and insects descending on paddy fields. The idea of the whole village turning vegetarian came from the wily old priest of the Sheetala temple. He has an axe to grind.'

'Sh! Sh!' Menaka was aghast at such blasphemous talk. 'Don't ever say such a thing again,' she whispered feverishly. 'The decree has come from Ma Sheetala herself. She appeared before Purohit Thakur, the temple priest, in a dream. She told him that a curse will fall on all those who violate it. They will be destroyed.'

'I don't believe Ma Sheetala said any such thing,' Larani protested. 'She would never be so cruel. All these decrees are given out by evil men. They turn the distress of ordinary people to their own advantage. They issue decrees and threaten those who disobey with dire consequences in the name of the gods.'

'Hai! Hai! Hai!' Menaka exclaimed with a shudder. 'I wonder that your tongue didn't fall out as you uttered those words. *Pregnant woman! Craved fish!* Shame on Subal Dom's wife and shame on you. Haven't you seen Muslims fast during the whole month of Ramzan? They don't even drink water. If they can, why can't we? And we haven't even been asked to fast. Only to give up fish and meat.'

'It is part of their religion…'

'The question of religion rises when people turn irreligious,' Menaka answered in a faraway voice. 'Don't you remember what happened during the great drought? Rain fell in torrents the very morning after the kirtan parties went round the village doing the naam gaan and all the yagnas and pujas were held. The gods punish sinning mortals with such scourges and remove them when they propitiate them with prayer and sacrifice. It's like when a pond is left unclean for years and the water gets polluted. What do we do? Don't we empty the whole pond, scrub it with lime and fill it with clean water? Why do we do this? Because we know that the pollution will spread to other ponds and skin diseases like boils, itches, sores and ringworm will afflict the villagers. Everyone knows this.'

With the start of the propitiation of the gods a kind of excitement gripped the villagers. The pujas, yagnas and continuous naam gaan brought a change in their drab lives. It was almost like a festival in which old and young participated equally. A wave of happiness passed over Larani the first morning as she woke to the sweet sounds of drums and cymbals. Rubbing her eyes, she ran to the door to see the village women, including her mother and aunts, standing with brass pots of water to offer obeisance to the kirtan singers as they passed in a procession. They would wash their feet and dry them with the anchals of their saris. This was a time-honoured custom in their village. Larani's lips curled in a snide smile. She wondered at the men's smug acceptance of the women's devotion and how easy it was to earn it. *If Pabna was here*, she thought, *he would say that he liked the sounds of kirtan singing because of the feast that would follow. That he went to the temple only for the prasad and loved looking at the image of Ma Sheetala because it was beautiful.*

The procession would start making rounds of the village before dawn and stop when the sun got too hot for comfort. They would then proceed to the paddy fields, put up a ceremonial platform made of stones and earth and plant a tulsi sapling beside it. No need to spray the paddy with pesticide, the temple priest had said, the smell of tulsi would drive all winged creatures away.

Morning waned into afternoon. The villagers were agog with excitement. Wherever she went, Larani found men, women and children standing in groups and talking in whispers, waiting for the miracle to happen. For the moment, when swarms of insects would rise from the fields and wing their way to other lands. Her eyes scanned the crowds. They sought a figure, long and lean, standing a head above the others like a young fan-palm in the middle of a paddy field. Her heart beat fast, her body was racked with sobs. She couldn't sleep. She woke shivering, every now and then, and wept bitterly for hours. She cursed herself for being so prim and prissy. Her beloved hadn't a clue to her feelings for him. *Next time he comes,* she decided, *I will open my heart to him. I will tell him what I feel; what I have felt for him ever since I was a little girl. If nothing else I'll be relieved of the secret burden I carry.*

The days went by, one by one. Prayers, yagnas and naam gaan went on in full swing but the paddy in the fields remained as weak and listless as ever. Breezes blew over the wilting stalks, the sun showered its beams and rain fell in generous showers. But they gave no sign of revival. Like consumptive patients, they seemed to have sunk in deep apathy.

Disregarding the temple priest's diktat, Kanai Maiti continued spraying his field with pesticide. He had visited the Block Development Office and learned all there was to learn about saving crops from insects. 'The man has gone mad,' the priest sniggered and announced at last. 'An ant grows wings just before its death. No one can save him now.'

It was on one of those days, when the whole village was gripped with doubt and uncertainty, that Pabna came home. He had been sick for weeks from a high fever. Pain wracked his limbs and he tottered every time he took a step. He had become so thin that the clothes hung from his limbs. The tall lissom youth had turned into a blackened, worm-eaten, dying stalk of paddy. Larani took one look at him and her heart sank like a stone in her chest.

'I was sick,' Pabna gasped between deep breaths, sinking to the ground before Larani. 'It's a miracle I survived. Only the blessings ... only the blessings of my parents...'

'Hush,' Larani whispered. Running into the house, she made a sherbet with sugar and lime leaves and held it to his lips. Pabna drank it in one swallow like a man who had just reached an oasis after crossing a mighty desert. Larani took the glass from his hands and continued gazing at him. 'What happened to *you*?' Pabna asked after a while. 'Why are you looking like a death's head? What does all this have to do with you?'

Larani smiled. 'I am sick too. A mysterious insect has found its way into my heart. It gnaws and nibbles at it all the time. Every minute of the day and night.' She sighed and went on, 'It's good that you have come home at last. Just in time to enjoy the festival.'

★

A week later. Dusk was falling, together with a slight drizzle not uncommon in the month of ashwin. Larani felt the droplets tumble from the leaves of the drumstick tree and wrap her in a gentle embrace as she crept stealthily into the yard where the old hen sat, brooding and clucking over her eggs. It was their only hen. Larani's mother hadn't sold it even when starvation stared them in the face. Larani had cherished a wish for months. She would kill it and cook the meat for Pabna when he came home. The sight of her lover's worn face and emaciated limbs had exacerbated the longing but her chance hadn't come. Her mother was at the bridge, tonight, listening to the naam gaan and she was alone in the house. The hand that held the knife trembled and her heart thudded dully as the distant sounds of drums and cymbals filled her ears.

Larani shut the door of the kitchen and started her cooking. She took great pains with it. She used up all the oil and spices left in the house and made a rich chicken curry. Then, when her work was done, she plucked a tiny mirror from a niche in the wall and began preparing for her tryst. She oiled her hair, combed it carefully, and twisted it into a khonpa. She scrubbed her face with a gamchha and lined her eyes with kajal. Decorating her high forehead with a dark brown catechu teep she held up the mirror. The face that looked back at her had all the sweet freshness of a healthy young paddy stalk. She could smell the fragrance that rose from her limbs. It was the scent of happiness.

Larani stepped on the path that led to Hola Burho's hut. A full moon danced and pranced in the sky above her head and stars shone, pure and white, like jasmine flowers. The faint humming of cicadas came to her ears as she walked carefully, the big bowl of chicken curry in her hands. The bowl was very hot. Her palms turned red and sweat poured from them. But she endured the burning and walked on. She was disobeying the orders given by the village elders but didn't feel a trace of fear. Pabna had been ill and needed nourishing food. That was the only thing that mattered. It was possible that someone would see her and complain to the Panchayat. She would be summoned, shamed and denounced. For all she knew her old mother's subsidy might be cut off as a punishment for her daughter's action. The possibility made her somewhat uneasy but could not make her change her mind.

Larani walked the village path on feet as light as wings. Her heart lifted with happiness. Her lips grew moist and her ears were filled with the singing of humming birds. Pabna had come home! What was more, he had recovered from his illness. He was getting better day by day. The old teasing smile had returned to his face. Peace and contentment swept over Larani's soul in gentle waves. Her face was irradiated in a secret smile.

But it vanished the moment she entered Hola Burho's hut and called out Pabna's name. When, instead of the one she sought, his old father hobbled out of the yard and exclaimed, 'Pabna? But he isn't home. He left for the Panchayat office in the evening. He should have returned long ago. I don't know what's keeping him…'

Larani's heart sank with disappointment but she shook it off with stoic resolution. *What better news could I've heard than that,* she told herself, *the fresh air of the village and the good home food his mother cooks for him, has worked wonders. He has recovered … so well recovered that he's gadding about like he used to in the old days.* It seemed to her, at that moment, that all her dreams were within her reach. She had woven these dreams from childhood. Through all the time she had sat by Pabna's side watching him at work, obeying his commands, preparing gaab for him and listening to him testing the beat of his khol. The time was near, very near, when their lives would be tied together like string to leather and their hearts beat in unison to the resonant rhythm of Ma Durga's drum.

She stepped on the path once more; this time in the direction of the Panchayat office. Suddenly a gust of wind, laden with dust and leaves, stopped her in her tracks. Her anchal slipped from her shoulder and trailed on the ground. As she stooped to pick it up, she felt an icy breath blow into her heart, nipping it like the prick of an insect. An eerie sensation, such as she had never known before, passed down her limbs. It frightened her. Her lips trembled and her feet lost their power. She stood still, looking up at the sky; unable to move. Then, with a mighty effort, she dragged her resisting body and paralysed feet to the bus station Pabna would pass on his way back. *I'll hand him the bowl as soon as I see him,* she thought, *we will go to the empty schoolroom where he can sit on the stone floor and eat in peace.*

The hours passed one by one. Pabna did not come. At last, weary of waiting, feeling bereft and unloved, she turned her steps towards the school. The compound was flooded with moonlight. The wind whistled through the banana clump that stood in a corner, bending its stems to the ground; tearing at its fronds. *Krrrr* ... the whirring of insects feeding on the grain was heard from the paddy fields.

As she walked towards the schoolroom a faint sound came to her ears. Larani was surprised. Who could be there at this time of night? She pricked up her ears. And now she heard them clearly. Pabna and Menaka were talking in hushed voices. It seemed to Larani that they had been together for a long, long time...

'Pabna-da,' she heard the fake anguish in Menaka's whispered plea, 'will I shrivel up and die like the paddy stalks?'

'Why do you say that?' A cautious hiss from Pabna.

'Because, like them, I too am being consumed. Thousands of insects are swimming in my blood. They are draining all the sap out of me. I'm afraid I'll die of the agony...'

Larani screamed. A long-drawn-out scream. No one heard her. Because at that moment an old Vaishnav, frenzied with Krishna love, began chanting Hare Krishna Hare Ram to the loud beats of his drum. Larani's heart-broken cry splintered in tiny crystals and melted in the autumn air.

Larani flung the bowl of meat on the wall of the schoolroom and ran. Her numb, powerless feet grew wings and flew over rocks and stones and thorns and brambles, not stopping till they reached her mother's hut. Flinging herself on the floor she dashed her limbs against it like a poisoned insect in the throes of death.

'Where have you been?' Her old mother, long returned from the naam gaan, looked at her curiously. 'It is late. Come and eat.'

Larani rose slowly to her feet. The thought of food nauseated her. But the entire village was participating in a festival and so was she. Fasting during this auspicious time would bring bad luck to the one she loved. Who occupied her thoughts all the time. For whose welfare she prayed day and night. How could she be so selfish?

Larani made a ball of rice and put it in her mouth. It smelt of the old hen she had killed and cooked, so richly, with oil and spices. The gorge rose to her throat but she pushed it down. And now tears, acid sharp, burned her eyes and fell, in slow drops, on the rice she was eating. *These are poison tears*, she murmured to herself, *they will save the paddy from harm. Each grain will remain fresh and whole; untouched by pillaging pests on this dark night of the insect festival.*

Notes on Contributors

Anil Ghorai was born in Rukminipur village in the East Medinipur district of West Bengal on 1 November 1957 and received his higher education from Krishnanagar College of Nadia district in West Bengal. His voice is considered one of the most prominent voices in the genre of Dalit fiction. He has authored seventy-four books in Bengali, English and Hindi. They comprise novels, short stories and children's books. Some of his best-known works are *Nunbari, Megh Jiboner Trishna, Jaadu Orhna, Aaguner Padavali* and *Shwetpadma*. He is the recipient of many prestigious awards and distinctions. Among them are Sanskriti Award (1991), Michael Madhusudan Award (1994), Tarashankar Award (2001), Bankim Smriti Puraskar (2010), and Dalit Sahitya Academy Puraskar. He died on 23 November 2014 in Kolkata.

Kalyani Thakur Charal was born in Bagula in the Nadia district of West Bengal in 1965 into a family from the Matua community. Her parents played an important role in her early upbringing by ensuring that she got an excellent education as well as instilling in her a pride in her womanhood. Today she is hailed as a prominent Dalit feminist writer of West Bengal.

She has published four volumes of poetry, a collection of short stories, a number of essays and an autobiography. Most of her works have been translated into English. She is also a well-known editor. She runs the Dalit women's magazine *Neer* and is on the board of a publishing house which focusses solely on Dalit writing. She is widely travelled and lives in Kolkata.

Mahasweta Devi, one of the most respected writers of Bengal, was born on 14 January 1926 in Dhaka, now in Bangladesh. A prominent writer and activist, her specialization lies in her studies of Adivasis, Dalits and other marginalized people of India. She has lived among Adivasis in several villages of West Bengal, Bihar, Madhya Pradesh and Chhattisgarh, and portrayed their struggles and dilemmas with first-hand knowledge and extraordinary sensitivity. She has written over 100 novels and twenty collections of short stories. Her works have been widely translated and she has been the recipient of several prestigious awards. Among them are Sahitya Akademi Award, Padma Shree, Padma Vibhushan, Jnanpith and the Ramon Magsaysay Award. One of her novels was shortlisted for the Man Booker Award and she was nominated for the Nobel Prize in 2012. Some of her best-known works are *Aranyer Adhikar, Agnigarbha, Stano Dayini, Hazaar Churasi'r Ma* and *Ullas*. She died in Kolkata on 28 July 2016.

Manohar Mouli Biswas was born into a Namashudra family in Khulna, now in Bangladesh, in 1943. Navigating a challenging trajectory marked by poverty and lack of exposure, he managed to overcome all the hurdles an unjust society placed in his path and attained an education. Today he enjoys the reputation of being one of the most prominent Dalit writers of West Bengal. His works comprise four volumes of poetry, a collection of short stories, seven essay anthologies and an autobiography titled *Aamar Bhubane Aami Benche Achhi*. He is currently the president of the Bangla Sahitya Sanstha and has steered the editorial direction of the groundbreaking bimonthly literary magazine, *Dalit Mirror*, for a decade. He lives in Kolkata and works as a staunch advocate for Dalit causes in West Bengal.

Manoranjan Byapari was born in 1951 in a Namasudra family of East Pakistan, now Bangladesh. The family moved to India when Manoranjan was three and lived in various refugee camps before finding permanent sanctuary in Kolkata. Hindered by financial constraints, Manoranjan did not receive a formal education and had to work as a rickshaw puller at one time. Yet, with extraordinary dynamism, he became a celebrated author, politician and activist with twelve novels, a hundred short stories and a number of essays to his credit. He is hailed as a pioneering author of Dalit literature of Bengal and is believed to have spearheaded the movement. His literary corpus documents the oppression and marginalization Dalits have suffered for generations in Bengal. His works have received recognition for the power and beauty of thought and language. He is the recipient of many awards and lives in Kolkata at present.

Nakul Mallik was born in November 1946 into a low-wage farming family of the Namasudra caste in Gajendra village of Khulna, now in Bangladesh. He was expected to carry on in the footsteps of his forefathers. But with his father's support he managed to get an education. He studied first in the village school, then moved to Kolkata for higher education. While still in school, his community's untouchable status started haunting him and the inhumanity displayed by the upper castes towards his people in Kolkata, took hold of his consciousness in a big way. The tragedy of Dalit existence moved him to write poems and stories in protest. He also wrote biographies of famous Dalits. Among his best-known works are *Bhaabna Chinta, Mukta Chinta, Babasaheb Ambedkar, Premer Golpo, Andoloner Golpo* and *Khoma Nei*. He lives in Kolkata.

Prafulla Kumar Roy was born on 11 September 1934 in Bikrampur, now in Bangladesh, and moved to India in 1950 as a refugee after the Partition of India. He is a prolific and celebrated author having written over 150 books including novels and short stories. His best-known work is the trilogy: *Keya Pata'r Nouko, Shatadharay Boye Jaye* and *Uttal Samudrer Itikatha*. These novels contain an analytical and sensitive exploration of life as lived by Bengali refugees in the aftermath of Independence. Many other novels from his vast output expose harsh and powerful realities in both rural and urban conditions. About forty-five telefilms, tele-series and features films have been made based on his novels. He resides in Kolkata.

Saratchandra Chattopadhyay was born on 15 September 1876 in the village of Debanandapur in West Bengal. A legendary author, he was a leading writer of his age, his popularity as a novelist outstripping even that of Rabindranath Tagore's. His novels have been translated into nearly all the regional languages of India and he is widely read all over the country to this day. His exploration of the female psyche and his examination of the dilemma women faced in nineteenth-century Bengali society is considered far ahead of the times. Among his best-known works are *Devdas, Parineeta, Srikanta, Palli Samaj* and *Pather Dabi*. His novels have been turned into films in many languages. Saratchandra died on 16 January 1935 but his literary legacy survives throughout India to this day.

Tarashankar Bandyopadhyay was born on 23 July 1898 in Labhpur village of West Bengal. A leading novelist of his times, he was a prolific writer. During his literary career he produced sixty-five novels, several short-story collections, plays and travelogues exploring various facets of human life in both rural and urban settings. Some of his best-known novels are *Arogya Niketan, Hanshuli Baank-er Upakatha, Ganadebata, Saptapadi, Bicharak* and *Kobi*. His works have been widely translated and many have been turned into successful films. Recipient of several awards like Rabindra Puraskar, Sahitya Akademi Award and the Jnanpith Award, he was honoured with the Padma Shri in 1962 and the Padma Bhushan in 1969. He died on 14 September 1971.